MW00439571

Finding Your Way

Finding Your Way

A Guide to Seminary Life and Beyond

PHILLIP G. CAMP

CASCADE *Books* • Eugene, Oregon

FINDING YOUR WAY
A Guide to Seminary Life and Beyond

Cascade Books
A Division of Wipf and Stock Publishers
199 W. 8th Ave., Suite 3
Eugene, OR 97401

www.wipfandstock.com

ISBN 13: 978-1-60608-252-2

Cataloging-in-Publication data:

Camp, Phillip G.

Finding your way : a guide to seminary life and beyond / Phillip G. Camp.

x + 110 p ; 23 cm

ISBN 13: 978-1-60608-252-2

1. Theological seminaries. 2. Theology—Study and teaching. 3 Seminarians—Religious life. I. Title.

BV4020 C4 2009

Manufactured in the U.S.A.

To my beautiful wife, Amy,

my partner in our Kingdom calling;

Words can never fully express my gratitude to her,

for her love and support through seminary life and beyond,

to this very day.

Contents

Acknowledgments

I WANT to thank those who contributed in a variety of ways to the making of this book. Several colleagues and former students, who are all good friends as well, read drafts of various stages of this book and offered helpful insights and suggestions for improvement. They are Megan Hackler, Aubrey Watkins, George Goldman, Josh Graves, Gary Holloway, Audrey Everson, Earl Lavender, and Lacey Rudisill. The administration of Lipscomb University awarded me a summer writing grant in 2007, which gave me the opportunity to complete the first draft of this book. I also want to thank Lee Camp for introducing me to the fine people at Wipf and Stock and for his encouragement. I am grateful to all those at Wipf and Stock/Cascade who have been very helpful in the process of publishing this book.

I am also grateful to the teachers, mentors, colleagues, and friends who aided me in my theological education and teaching, in a variety of ways. Their wisdom was a valuable resource to draw upon for this book. These include Randy Harris, Jerrie Barber, Terry Briley, Diogenes Allen, Mike Moss, Mark Black, Cecil and Dot Sherman, and, once more, Gary Holloway and Earl Lavender.

Finally, I want to express my deep appreciation to all of those people who contributed to my own theological education in so many ways, especially my wife, Amy, my parents, Jim and Edith Camp, and my in-laws, Bob and Leah Davis.

Needing Directions

Why I Wrote This

I DO not possess an innate sense of direction. When I know where I need to be, I can generally get there, though often in a roundabout way. I make wrong turns, go the opposite way I am supposed to, circle back, and drive until something looks familiar. It also does not help that I am slightly near-sighted, making street signs difficult to see, but I am too vain to wear my glasses. Likewise, I am too embarrassed or vain (two sides of the same coin?) to stop and ask for directions (yes, I fit the stereotype). Even if I have been there before, or if someone has given me directions, it is no guarantee that I will get to where I am going very quickly. When I finally find my way to a place, I will continue to take the same route even if it is the long way around, simply because it is now familiar.

My struggle with finding my way while driving is an apt metaphor for my theological education, and I suspect for many others' as well. When I started the study of Scripture, theology, practical theology, church history, and so on, I had a general sense of where I needed to go but little clue about how to find my way there. I often found myself lost in twists and turns of jargon and presuppositions that were unfamiliar to me. I saw things in a particular, and admittedly at times distorted, way. I was often embarrassed to ask questions or get help because I assumed everyone else was way ahead of me and were already headed in the right direction.

I remember vividly my first day in my first seminary class, which was on the Corinthian letters. A guy next to me was reading out of his Greek New Testament with no English Bible in sight. The danger alert in my head began to sound: *"Warning! Warning! Entering hostile territory with alien life forms!"* Shortly into that first class, the same student asked a question—one of those questions where you sensed he already knew the answer—that went something like, "Is this an example of over-realized eschatology in Paul?" Over-realized *what*?! Is that in the Greek? I felt at that moment that I was way out of my league and did not belong there, despite a sense of call to ministry. Either God or I had made a mistake. It turned out, upon eventually engaging in conversation with other students in the class, that this Greek-reading, jargon-spouting student was the exception rather than the rule. Still, that sense of lostness often dogged me during my theological education. Perhaps my upbringing in a conservative church (in most every sense of the word) enhanced that feeling, since the issues raised in my classes challenged many of my dearly held assumptions about the Bible and the church. If any of this sounds familiar, then I am writing for you.

After two master's degrees (master of arts in religion at a more theologically conservative institution and master of divinity from a mainline denomination's seminary) and a doctorate in Old Testament from a mainline seminary, I have moved to the other side of the podium. I now teach at the school where I earned my first master's degree. Here I frequently see in my students the same lostness and confusion that I had experienced. (Admittedly, it could be that I am losing and confusing them). On the other hand, I often see a confidence in other students, who believe they know exactly what they need to function in the ministry they intend to practice. So, in my classes, I find myself repeatedly offering the same advice, trying to build confidence in some of my students while challenging the unhealthy cockiness of others. Since I keep saying the same things over and over, I thought it might be helpful to write some of it down. If I experienced these things and if my students experience them, then I suspect that other theological students do as well.

Therefore, this book is written for theological students and those teaching theological students. Mostly I have in mind seminarians, but since, in some denominations, ministerial education is primarily received on the undergraduate level, I write for those students as well. I realize that not everyone who gets a theological education plans to enter "the ministry." I certainly do not believe that only those who are in paid, specialized ministry work are ministers. But in this book I have in mind primarily those who will work in congregational, para-church, or other service ministries. However, I hope that there is something helpful here for every theological student.

What follows arises out of my experiences both in my own theological education and as an educator of theology students. I talk about what I found helpful and what, with the benefit of hindsight, I wish I had done. I also draw on the wisdom and experience of my teachers, colleagues, and students, as well as other writers.[1] I offer my own little book with the

---

1. I found Helmut Thielicke's *A Little Exercise for Young Theologians* (Grand Rapids: Eerdmans, 1962; reprinted 1998) especially beneficial in my own theological education. If you are familiar with the book, you

simple intention of helping you find your way through your theological education.

Much of what I say deals directly with the educational experience, but at other times I have my eye on how what is done in school translates into what is done in the churches or other ministries. Therefore, while I consider this primarily an offering for students, I also see it as a gift for the churches if it in any way helps those who will one day serve those churches. Also, by dividing the book into parts dealing with the academic, spiritual, and church sides of seminary life, I do not mean to imply that these can or should be separated. As will be clear in what follows, all three are integrally related.

A final note on style: I generally address you, the reader, directly. That is, I use "you" a lot, which I was taught not to do in academic writing. But this is not academic writing. By doing so, I am not implying that everyone who reads this has all the same issues. Nor am I accusing. Once in my doctoral program I addressed a MDiv class on the prophetic ministry. When I ran a draft of my lecture by the teacher of the class, he suggested I replace "you" with "one" or some similarly non-direct reference. I did so then because it was his class. But here I am imagining that I am addressing my own students directly, so "you" seems appropriate. If one is offended by this, I beg one's forgiveness and hope it will not cause one to dismiss the whole book out of hand.

Your journey and mine through theological education will not be the same. It can hardly be since we all start at different places and encounter different detours and roadblocks. Still, I pray that this book can at least orient you in a helpful

---

will no doubt hear echoes of it in my writing here. If you are not familiar with it, I recommend it to you.

direction as you navigate your own theological journey. I pray that you do not fall asleep at the wheel (or while reading this book!) and, especially, that you do not give up on the journey. Finally, I pray that God will bless you on your own journey through seminary life and beyond.

PART ONE

Finding Your Way Academically

2

Remember *Who* You Are *Really* Working For

PERHAPS IT is a bit presumptuous here to assume why any given student might enter theological study. Some want to find answers to questions and longings deep within. Others enter theological study to simply spend another few years in school, putting off the repayment of student loans and getting a job. Some may be pressured by family expectations, being the pastor-designate of the family. Perhaps some are looking for faith or a deeper understanding of their faith. But my remarks here are largely addressed toward those who enter theological study out of a sense of calling (even if the calling is not yet defined).

It is easy to lose sight of why you entered this program of study, especially as time wears on. The initial excitement of engaging Scripture and theology, of learning to preach and teach, of dialoguing with other students on intellectually and spiritually stimulating topics often gives way to the toil of study. Greek and Hebrew paradigms, historical figures and dates, and various Christologies have to be learned. A few papers and hundreds of pages of reading are due *every week*! Exams come along, and lo and behold, they are far more difficult than what you experienced in high school and college.[1]

1. I try to remind my graduate students that a master's program should be more challenging and more difficult than their undergraduate programs. To adapt a line from Tom Hank's character, the baseball

9

Drowning in a sea of books, lecture notes, assignments, and exams, the student may declare concerning his or her call, as the prophet Jeremiah did, "You deceived me Lord, and I was deceived" (Jeremiah 20:7). Or, to paraphrase, "God, when you called me, this is *not* what I was signing up for."

It is in these moments that you must remember you are where you are precisely because you are called by God, who is preparing you for a special role in service to his church. Do not understand "special" here as intending a superior or more important role than other roles in the church (see 1 Corinthians 12). However, your calling does require special training. The intense study and demands of your theological education are not simply add-ons or hoops to get through before you can start the real business of the ministry that God has in store for you. They are what you are called to in this moment and are shaping you to continue another phase of your calling once you finish school. Furthermore, it is indeed God who has called you, and so you must respond faithfully to God's call. Thus, you should understand your theological training as part of your calling or vocation.

Some students forget for whom they are working not because of the burdens of study but because they are driven to succeed academically. I am not denigrating hard work at all, but some students find their whole self-worth in how well they do academically and how well they do in comparison to other students. I know this, because I was one of those students. While I always maintained in my mind that I was

---

manager Jimmy Dugan, in *A League of Their Own*, when one of his players was contemplating quitting because playing professional ball was getting too demanding: "Of course a master's program is hard. If it wasn't, everybody would do it."

studying for Jesus (and on some level I was), honest reflection tells me that I also wanted to be the best student because it would reflect well on me. "This little light of mine, I'm gonna let it shine"—on me! And given the nature of many of our seminaries, where simple academic achievement can be honored more than spiritual formation or service to the church, my grade-driven life was rewarded.

The cost, however, was high as I began to believe my own press, and the focus remained more on me than on God's calling. I often saw other students, fellow Christians, as competition rather than partners in God's mission, even resenting those who performed better than I did. My sense of worth rested in my ability to achieve rather than the fact that I am a child of God. I was condescending toward "lesser intellects," even avoiding their company while seeking the company of those whose company would reflect well on me. That is, I could be unloving and rude to "normal" folk while sucking up to teachers or the intellectual crowd. This is not at all to imply that all (or even most) of those teachers and intellectual types were afflicted with my sense of self-importance and self-centeredness. But it was easy for me to lose focus on the One who called me and fail to give him the glory. I would have done well to have kept Paul's words before me: "And whatever you do, whether in word or deed, do it all in the name of the Lord Jesus, giving thanks to God the Father through him" (Colossians 3:17).

3

You Do Not Know What You Need

"WHY DO we need all of this theology, Bible backgrounds, hermeneutics, and church history? I just want to go out and be Jesus to people." So goes, with variations, a typical complaint my colleagues and I hear from some of our students. Indeed, in our more honest moments, we might confess that we once made similar complaints. So much of the theological curriculum, at least in the moment, seems irrelevant to "real ministry." While practical theology or ministry courses might be appreciated because what is learned there can transfer almost immediately into church practice, it is harder for students to see how knowing who the Jebusites were, or various views on soteriology, or who wrote the Pentateuch, or Greek verb paradigms have anything to do with church life in the twenty-first century. Of course, we on theological faculties deserve some blame for failing to make clear why these topics matter to ministry and how they relate to one another.

To those students with these concerns, let me say this (hear a loving tone here): *You do not know what you need.* There is a great deal of presumption for a twenty-something student or someone who has never served day in and out in a church or ministry to say, "This doesn't really matter."

The curriculum in most theological schools was fashioned with much care and thought, taking into account the collective wisdom of the church. The church has said this is what we think is important in forming our ministers. Indeed, in a number of schools, the faculty members (at least many of them) served churches before coming to teach and remain deeply involved in the life of the church as pastors, Sunday school teachers, deacons, ministry leaders, etc. In those roles, they too recognize the needs of the church that are not immediately obvious to the student.

A good way to test my claim is simply to try to get a ministry position without the formal training. A few may succeed in doing so, but overall most will not have much luck. Why? Again, because the churches and ministries recognize that those who serve them need to develop certain skills and knowledge, as well as the ability to think theologically.

As for the desire to simply "be Jesus," one could respond, "Okay, but which Jesus?" The Jesus who's the friend, the friend next to you, and who really doesn't care what you do as long as you are nice to people? The Jesus who calls for plucking out eyes and cutting off hands? The human-looking Jesus who is just pretending to be like us? The fiery-eyed, sword-tongued Jesus in the blood-drenched robe?[1] Incomplete views of Jesus and heretical understandings of him (usually drawn from incomplete views) pervade the history of the church and extend into this very day (most contemporary heresies are simply retreads of earlier heresies). How does the minister discern who Jesus is and teach his/her congregation to do likewise? I suggest the answer comes in studying the history and theology of the church

1. For this one, see Revelation 19:11–16.

across time and in learning the content of Scripture and skills for hearing that content as a word to the church.

I regret that so many of my students have seen their theological education as merely a hoop to jump through in order to get to "real" ministry. As I have already suggested, a more helpful view of their ministry would be to see their theological training as part of their vocation, as the means by which they participate in God's kingdom *now* even as they anticipate their later participation.

For my first few years of teaching, I taught "Critical Introduction to the Bible," which many students dreaded because it was academically demanding, and it challenged their cherished beliefs. Students at times complained that the material was irrelevant or that it would not serve their ministries in any practical way. I told them (lovingly, of course) that they were too inexperienced to know what would or would not be relevant in ministry. I also invited them to come back in ten years and let me know whether it proved to be relevant or not. If enough former students found the course was irrelevant in their ministries, we could change it or get rid of it. Though no one has hit the ten year mark yet, those who do report back (with only one exception I can think of) have told me that the course material proved beneficial or that they wished they had paid better attention because they can now see the value. I am not so naïve as to think this is the universal experience of all the students in that course, but it is telling how, for so many of them, what seemed impractical at first has shown itself to be worthwhile over time.

Having said all of that, I will offer this caveat: some of what you do in your theological program will be irrelevant, but you will not know that for a while either. Sometimes teachers get stuck in ruts of teaching what we have always taught without considering whether how or what we teach serves today's students, who will serve today's church. Sometimes we get caught up in the academic side of things and, whether we realize it or not, divorce the subject matter from the life of the church (sometimes because we are more concerned with academic kudos than we are with serving the church). So please, the invitation stands: come back in ten years and tell us what was useful and what was not. Hopefully, your denomination, its seminaries, and their faculties are constantly reexamining how they train their ministers and making revisions along the way.

4

Read Your Bible

IF SOMEONE preparing to enter seminary asked me for one piece of advice, I think it would be, "Read your Bible, carefully and all the way through, before you begin." Then my unsolicited follow-up advice would be, "And keep reading it!" This may sound a bit obvious for someone who is going to spend two, three, or more years in theological study. You may well respond, "I will have to read the Bible all the time for my classes." Still, I offer this suggestion for a number of reasons.

First, you may not actually read the Bible all of the time for your classes. It is amazing how, in some programs, you can manage to get through without actually reading much of the Bible. Indeed, I suspect your assignments will include many more readings *about* the Bible than readings *in* the Bible itself. Or, perhaps more often you will be assigned bits and pieces of the Bible rather than long, sustained readings that give you some sense of the individual message of each book of the Bible and a grasp of the flow of the overall biblical narrative.

Second, biblical illiteracy within our churches remains a problem, even among denominations that once prided themselves on biblical knowledge. Thus, more and more students are coming into their theological education with little or no idea of what is in the Bible. They may know, or think they know, the gist of the Bible. But what many actually have is a conglomeration of images and stories from popular religious writers, television, and movie versions of biblical stories, and a general sense of what the Bible ought to say. That is, if I ask them to tell me about the Bible's account of Moses and the exodus, rather than the biblical story, they are likely to give me a composite portrait of Charlton Heston, the animated *Prince of Egypt*, and bits and pieces from a History Channel discussion of Moses "as he really was." So, to state the obvious, the best way to know what the Bible actually says is to read it.

Third, biblical literacy is important because it is foundational to the other disciplines within your theological education. All churches claim to respect biblical authority and to develop their belief and practice from the authoritative teaching of Scripture. So, ideally, systematic theology, practical theology, pastoral theology, and of course Old Testament and New Testament theology should be rooted in reflection on Scripture. I say "ideally," because in practice this is clearly not always the case. I remember a theology class in seminary where a professor made her theological point, claiming to base it on a particular biblical text. A student (not me!) in the class pointed out that the text she cited did not actually say what she said it did, and the teacher began to fumble for words to recover her point. The issue was not that she cited the wrong book, chapter, and verse; the issue was that she misrepresented what the text actually said. Most of the other students simply took the professor at her word because they did not know the Bible well enough to test her claims (or were too intimidated to challenge her). You can test your professors' teachings and your own theological understandings against Scripture only if you know Scripture.

Fourth, reading your Bible allows you to make inter-biblical connections and to understand Scripture as a whole. Once you begin to know the content of Scripture fairly well, you begin to see a vast web of interconnections within the Bible. Texts allude to, play off of, and respond to other texts. For example, chords struck in Deuteronomy resound throughout Joshua, Judges, 1 and 2 Samuel, 1 and 2 Kings, and Jeremiah, as well as much of the New Testament. You almost cannot help hearing Deuteronomy in these books, if you know what to listen for.

Furthermore, it is almost impossible to read the New Testament intelligently without a thorough knowledge of the Old Testament. So much of the New Testament simply assumes the Old Testament background. This became obvious to me when I spent a summer in Russia in the early 1990s, between my first and second master's programs. The Iron Curtain had just come down, and various Christian groups were flooding Russia with New Testaments.[1] So most of the Russians I worked with that summer had only New Testaments, and what I quickly discovered was that so much of the New Testament was a mystery to them because of the Old Testament references and allusions that are not explained, whether it be people (e.g., Ruth, Elisha, Jonah, Adam, and Eve), images and symbols (e.g., the Passover lamb, the

1. Apparently it was quicker and more cost efficient to print New Testaments than the entire Bible, and the teachings of some denominations so elevate the New Testament that they, at least in practice, do not assign any particular importance to the Old Testament. This, of course, misses the fact that the church canonized the Old and New Testaments together as Christian Scripture.

ark of the covenant, or the serpent), or events (e.g., the flood, Sodom and Gomorrah, or the exodus from Egypt). To my surprise, when I began teaching, I found precisely the same void in most of my students' knowledge, even those who were raised in church.

Fifth, the Bible tells the story of which we are a part. It helps us put things in order, know the key players and events, see the patterns, and find our place in the story. I am surprised how many students struggle to put the key events in order. It is a story they claim is primary for understanding God's purposes for them, yet they do not know the story.

Sixth, reading the Bible allows us to appreciate the diversity of Scripture. While God's purpose to redeem Creation provides an overarching theme, there is a great deal of diversity within the unity of Scripture; a symphony of voices. However, the multi-faceted ways of understanding who God is and how God interacts with Creation are lost if one does not know Scripture as a whole. In addition, the many voices of Scripture, once they are heard, should invite a theological humility that recognizes that no single biblical description of God or God's relationship with Creation is sufficient or can be absolutized. A broad reading of Scripture both enriches and constantly challenges human ways of conceiving God, including our theologies.

So develop a regular discipline of reading large portions of Scripture. Read through the books, several chapters at a time, in order to hear the messages of those books. Read slowly enough to see the details, but in your contemplation of the details, don't miss the forest for the trees.[2] Read all

2. This suggestion is not intended as a rejection of more contemplative forms of reading, such as *lectio divina*, that focus on very select

of Scripture, Genesis through Revelation, to hear the whole counsel of Scripture and to avoid cycling through a few select texts or books that immediately delight but do not ever challenge you. Read apart from any biblical readings you are assigned for classes. Let your larger reading inform the more narrow readings you have to do for classes. And, of course, read with the intention of hearing God through Scripture.

Finally, make reading Scripture a lifelong discipline, because you will see and hear new things in every journey through the Bible. I can still picture my grandfather sitting in his recliner reading his well-worn King James Bible. He read and reread the Bible as long as I knew him. Especially after he retired, he would read through the Bible multiple times in a year. He told me that he learned or saw something new every time. Avail yourself of the ever-new riches of God's revelation in Scripture, and enjoy the constant journey of discovery and the constant challenges that come in engaging God's word in Scripture and being engaged by God through Scripture.

---

portions of Scripture. However, it seems to me that *lectio divina* and such methods of reading are better served once a person has a general understanding of Scripture. Otherwise, the temptation may be to concentrate on only portions of Scripture that we especially like or, because our reading is so narrow, to come to idiosyncratic or, dare I say it, incorrect understandings of the text by decontextualizing it.

5

Manage Your Time Well

FOR MANY of you, that dreaded time will come when you have three papers, a presentation, a translation, and an exam all due on the same day. You will wonder how it crept up on you so quickly and how in the world you will get it all done. You will thank God for inexpensive coffee and curse yourself for needing it as you cloister yourself in the library by day and then reel off a series of all-nighters in your room.

A friend of mine, who also teaches, refers to this student habit of waiting until the last minute to write papers as the "eschatological view of paper writing." That is, the student hopes the Lord will return before the paper is due, and so does not begin until the last minute. Why waste all that time if writing the paper proves unnecessary? Of course the gamble here, as many students know, is that the Lord may not return as a thief in the night on the night before the paper is due. At least he hasn't yet. Surely there is a better way.

It may be helpful to note why students fall behind. In part, they do so because there are so many day to day assignments, plus internship requirements, plus church obligations, plus family or personal matters, plus those minor little things like eating and sleeping. In part, it can also have to do with unexpected emergencies. But for many students, much of it has to do with not planning ahead. If three papers are due on the same day and it takes twenty-plus hours to write one of them (I will let you decide if the estimate is too high or too low), simple math tells you that you will not get all of this done in a day or two. Of course, for many students, the solution is to beg for extensions. But I am not sure we teachers do you a favor by granting extensions (except in emergencies) since this only reinforces the cycle of putting things off. I had a professor in seminary who refused to grant extensions—period. His reasoning was that Sunday came every week, whether we future pastors were ready for it or not. Thus, demanding that things be turned in on time was a means of disciplining us for our church work.

One way to help with this problem is to discipline yourself in the use of your time. That is, make and stick to a schedule. You might want to invest in a day planner or calendar for this, unless you have a *really* good memory. Then you will need to look at your days, months, and the semester as a whole and set priorities about what comes first, second, . . . forty-second, etc. I also found it helpful to stick up notes reminding me of what is coming up or what is due. That, of course, was in the dark ages. Now you can set alarms on your computers or phones to remind you. You will have to figure out a system that works for you.

Your daily schedule should include devotional and prayer time, classes, study time, some time for exercise, meals, and sleep. And yes, by all means, work in some time just to play (though this should not take up the bulk your time while you are in school). Section off the day by hours and lay out your day, building it around your class schedule during the week. Look the schedule over and if more than 75 percent of the time is filled with naps and ping-pong or computer games, consider reworking it a bit.

With respect to meals and sleep, both are important for your mental and physical health while in school. Sufficient sleep and eating well will help you work and study far more efficiently than repeated nights of four hours sleep and sodas and candy bars for meals. You will have to make up the sleep somewhere anyway, and my experience is students who do not get it at night get it in my classroom, which (inexplicably!) affects their class performance. And caffeine and sugar can only get you so far.

You will also need to look at what will be due in all of your courses each month and at the end of the semester, including exam dates. Take a look at your syllabi. In most cases, you will find due dates and exam dates. Armed with this valuable information, you can plan ahead. If two papers are due on the same day, you can start research and writing early enough to have them done on time. If two exams are on the same day, you can start studying earlier.

I realize that I am tilting at windmills here. The cramming, all-nighter culture is firmly ingrained in the psyche of most students. And, to be honest, most muddle through, pass their classes, and get their degrees. But I would like to suggest that theological education, as training for ministry, should call us to more than muddling through or mere academic survival (really this is the case for any vocation God has given us). What you study matters for the life of the church you will serve or whatever other vocation your degree is preparing you for, and you have been granted the privilege and responsibility to prepare for that vocation. What you get through your theological education will serve as tools for the rest of your life. Disciplining yourself to give sufficient time and attention to your education will go a long way in helping you continue to use those tools wisely and responsibly to the glory of God.

6

Grades Do and Don't Matter

D<small>O GRADES</small> matter in theological study? Well, yes and no. I think theology students (and students in general!) often stress out too much over getting the A and so miss the joy of learning and the adventure of taking risks in the pursuit of knowledge. The result of a theological education should not be that you have so stressed yourself out over grades that, by the time you are done, you hate study and learning. Study is an ongoing part of ministry, and your goal now is preparation and formation for ministry, not a certain GPA. Grades do matter to some extent because most schools require a minimum GPA to stay in school. But, otherwise, education and formation is more important than simply getting good grades.

Grades are an indication either of comparative achievement in a class (though few actually grade in this way anymore) or a measure of mastery of material. While the latter can affect one's ministry, overall I think there is little direct correlation between a GPA and effectiveness in ministry. That is, God regularly uses B and C students (and even ones who flunk out!) in powerful ways, just as he does A students.

I will also say, however, that while grades are not necessarily a predictor of effectiveness in ministry, they can indicate something about a student's work ethic. If you were a candidate for a ministry position at my church and I was on the search committee, I would have far less interest in your grades than in how conscientiously you went to class, did your work, and *prepared* for exams. My questions would have far more to do with your work ethic than your GPA. To me, how conscientiously you did your work in school provides a helpful indication of how seriously you will take your ministry work.

You might respond, "But I do work hard in classes that interest me or on assignments that I think really matter for my future ministry."[1] Fine. But what I will hear is, "I am one who works hard when it suits me or when I like what I am doing, but who slacks off when I don't care for the assignment." The bad news here is that often in ministry work you will have to do things that are not interesting or that you do not want to do. The question becomes whether you will demonstrate the same work ethic in those situations as in the ones you enjoy.

It is also true that, given your workload, you sometimes have to make decisions about where to invest time. Part of this requires discipline to organize your time in order to accomplish all that is required of you. Apart from wasting time, however, no matter how much you do, you could always do more. Let's face it. In the study of theology, we are already starting out about 2000 years behind, and there will always be one more thing we could read or one more thing to learn. One of my professors, who insisted on high quality work, told me that I eventually had to quit researching and start writing. There was always one more note I could chase down and, perhaps, marginally improve the paper. But to get the paper done

1. Refer back to Chapter 3, "You Do Not Know What You Need."

and study for the next exam and finish my Hebrew readings, I had to settle for not exhaustively researching the paper. So tasks must be weighed, time and energy invested where most needed (even if it means giving less attention to something else), and *the consequences accepted*. That is, to make an A or B in one class, you may have to accept a B or C in another, especially if there are other demands on your time such as family or work.

A word on requesting special favors is also in order here. Frequently my colleagues and I hear pleas for deadline extensions, extra credit,[2] adding points, or the like as a student tries to improve his or her grade. At the very least, by asking you run the risk of looking undisciplined or immature. Of course, true emergencies arise that can affect your schoolwork (e.g., sick children, death in the family, personal injury). However, I think these requests for favors are often ways of covering a poor work ethic. Students' lack of discipline comes back to bite them. In these cases, the adult thing to do is to accept the consequences. Indeed, teachers can encourage such poor behavior by regularly bumping grades, giving extra credit, or granting extensions. This behavior will then likely spill over into the students' ministries.

Also, I get especially bothered when students invoke "grace" as a cover for their lack of discipline. That is, they ask for grace in grading, counting on me to realize that, after all, we are all Christians here. This cheapens grace. Certainly God's grace covers our failings, but grace is not to be an excuse to develop bad habits. Grace actually works in the other

2. One definition I have heard for "extra credit" (though I do not remember where I heard it) is "rewarding students for not doing the work they were supposed to have done."

direction, empowering us to be what God has called us to be. Furthermore, whether students realize it or not, sometimes the gracious thing to do, both for the students and the churches or ministries they will one day serve, is to make them accept the consequences of their actions and allow them to learn from those consequences.

Finally, in all of this, keep in mind that all we say and do is to the glory of God—including our schoolwork. A good question to constantly ask yourself, not to produce guilt but as honest self-examination, is, "Am I honoring Christ and his church in my schoolwork?" If the answer is "yes," then the grades themselves are really unimportant.

7

Be Careful with Labels

ARLY IN my theological education I cut myself off from valuable avenues of learning because I had preconceptions of who the good guys and the bad guys were, theologically speaking. Without seriously considering the *merit* of their positions, I wrote off others' views because, in my mind, I had classified them as "liberal" or "postmodern." I did not really have either of these terms well-defined. In general, I understood liberals as those who did not believe the Bible was true in a literal and historical sense; postmoderns were those who did not believe in truth at all. I was usually able to lump my teachers and authors we read into one or both of these camps based on such clear and unassailable criteria as where they went to church, who published their books, and whether they believed what I believed about various matters. To be fair, I also had a category for the ultra-conservatives and fundamentalists, who were not as progressive or enlightened as I was.

Of course, the practical reason for lumping scholars and their books into these categories was that it allowed me to dismiss their arguments without ever actually engaging them. Neither liberals nor fundamentalists deserved a hearing because everyone knows what they think. Moreover, because they were liberals or fundamentalists or (add your favorite pejorative label here), whatever they thought had to be wrong. If only everyone were sensible like me.

I will admit that when I left my first master's program at a fairly "conservative" school in my own denomination to attend a "liberal" school of another denomination, I had some sense that I was going as a spy into an enemy camp, looking to undermine their ungodly positions. Then something strange happened. As I was exposed to the teachings of these "liberals," in classes and in books, it became increasingly clear to me that, by far, most of these people loved Jesus and were deeply concerned for the church. That is, they really believed! Even if we saw things differently at times, we had the same larger ultimate concerns and we confessed Jesus's lordship in our lives.

As you go through your theological education, wherever you are on the theological spectrum, please be cautious about applying labels to others, or even to yourself. Admittedly, categorizing other people's views or positions is sometimes a necessary expedient, but try to have some sense of what the labels mean and to use them without a sneer or scowl. It is amazing how many connotations there are for words like "liberal," "conservative," "postmodern," "fundamentalist," or "evangelical." Too often their meanings are moving targets because they are applied relative to the convictions of whoever is using them. That is, anyone to the left of me is a liberal and anyone to the right a conservative, or if you move far enough right, a fundamentalist.

Please do not use such labels simply to dismiss the arguments of others without seriously considering them. Never use them to demonize others. Perhaps the latter is the greater danger in applying such labels because we do not simply disregard what others say, but we judge their faith and motivations. In my own classes, I sometimes make use of the labels to characterize theological positions or views on Scripture, but I also try to make it clear, for example, that "liberal" does not equal "unbelief" or that "conservative" does not equal "biblicism" or "bibliolatry."

I am not suggesting that theological and philosophical differences are unimportant, but, believe it or not, conservatives can learn from liberals and liberals from conservatives. Postmoderns can learn from moderns and moderns from postmoderns. In my experience as a student in schools of differing theological leanings, "liberal" and "conservative" teachers and students forget this.

One of my seminary teachers passed on to us the advice of one of her teachers; advice that I think serves any theological student (really anyone) well. She said that when we prepare to engage in discussion or debate with people whose views differ from ours, we should study their position so well that we could present it back to them so they would respond, "That is exactly what I am saying." Even if we still do not agree, at least we have given the other point of view a fair hearing and, hopefully, have developed some sympathy for the one holding the position.

In the process of listening and seriously considering other views, you just might expand your understanding a bit. Who knows? You might even change your mind on some things in the process, which is not a bad thing. If nothing else, by seriously engaging other positions, rather than labeling in order to dismiss them, we are forced to reexamine our own. We also learn to respect the fact that well-intentioned, sincere, honest people can consider the same information or issue, study it closely, and come away with different conclusions.

This is not to suggest that there is no such thing as heresy, but it is to suggest that someone is not a heretic by the mere fact that he or she disagrees with you or me. This is not a call either to abandon your views or to say all views are right or equal. It is a call not to pigeonhole others and to consider that others could have something valuable to say to you.

Finally, there is the spiritual dimension to think about in such labeling. First, as I noted above, the labels we use are often applied relative to where we stand. Thus, I make myself the center and arbiter of right and wrong, good and bad. And putting oneself in such a position is usually spiritually precarious. Second, when I simply write off someone using labels, without actually listening to him or her, I violate both the second greatest command—to love my neighbor as myself (Matthew 22:39)—and the golden rule—to do to others as I would have them do to me (Matthew 7:12). Thus, such uses of labels to dismiss others serve to destroy rather than build Christian community.

8

Ask Questions

I HAVE often heard that there are no dumb questions. In one of my schools, that assertion was made by a reassuring administrator during orientation. Next, a somewhat blunter professor spoke to us and disagreed with the administrator. He told us, "There are dumb questions. But you won't know them till you ask them." Maybe it is the fear of being seen as dumb or revealing our ignorance that keeps us from asking questions. We may assume that we should have known the answer or that everyone but us knows the answer already or is satisfied with the answers being given, so we clam up. However, it is precisely because of ignorance that students should ask questions. Why assume that you ought to know already what you have come to school to learn (unless of course you have not been paying attention or doing your assignments)? One of the time-proven methods of getting information you do not have is to ask someone who does know. You may even discover that a number of other students have the same questions but are likewise afraid to ask.

Becoming educated in any field involves more than simply receiving information. It involves processing and considering the information received. It involves seeking clarification when lectures or readings are unclear. It involves pursuit of the subject matter beyond the stated requirements of the syllabus. It involves testing various perspectives (including your teachers'!) against the facts and against each other in order to come to some reasonable conclusion. Asking questions demonstrates both your engagement with the subject and your desire to seek understanding. It is not a challenge to the credentials, intelligence, or integrity of the teacher. Only the most arrogant teacher could think that his or her views are unquestionable. Of course, you will discover that a few teachers take any question as a challenge, and such teachers have a knack for shutting down discussion immediately: "Well, all learned people in the field agree with this." When you have such teachers, keep in mind that you can let your questions lead you to your own search for alternative views, whether you get to air them in class or not.

Sometimes good teachers will push you to pursue the answers to your questions on your own. Indeed, asking questions is not a way to avoid doing the work of study, nor is it a substitute for failing to do assignments or for paying attention in classes. I had one teacher whose opinion I greatly respected. So after I moved on to another stage in my theological education, I would come to him with my questions from classes in my new school. I noticed that he rarely answered my questions directly; he usually gave me a list of books to read. Finally, perhaps somewhat frustrated with me, he said, "I know how much someone wants an answer by what he is willing to do to get it." My translation of this was: "Stop coming to me looking for the right answers. Learn to find the answers by doing the necessary hard work and coming to your own conclusions." That is, sometimes he did not answer so as not to short-circuit my own exploration and thinking on the matter.

Keep in mind as well, that there are some questions that are better not asked. Avoid questions beginning with "Do we have to know?" The is a sure-fire way to communicate to your teacher that you are not looking so much to learn as to get by with the least effort possible. If your teacher has said it or if it is in your reading assignments, assume that you have to know it. Note also that some people ask questions to hear themselves talk and to show, though their words are phrased as a question, that they already know the answer. Such questions often begin with "Isn't it true that….?" Okay, I will admit it. I was often that student. What I have found is that most teachers appreciate good questions that are truly an attempt to explore an issue further. On the other hand, teachers often try to avoid eye contact or pretend they do not see the raised hands of those students who have a habit of asking simply to hear themselves talk or to show off what they know.

So ask and seek. Developing a spirit of inquiry will help in your training now and will put you on a lifelong path of "faith seeking understanding,"[1] which will surely bless you and those you serve in your ministry.

1. See the preface and first chapter of Anselm's *Proslogion*.

9

Think

SUGGESTING THAT you think seems like a fairly obvious piece of advice for a student. However, it has been my experience as a student and a teacher that, not to put it too sharply, far less thinking goes on in the course of getting an education than you might think. I have had those teachers who required me to state a view and defend it or wrestle through a problem or issue. But equally as often, teachers required me simply to repeat back on exams what they said in class or what I read in a book. Unfortunately, too often in my own teaching, I have been guilty of the same thing. Even when I attempt to have my students consider the options on an issue, take a position, and defend it, many cannot do it. They have been so conditioned to regurgitate that they get a case of the dry heaves when forced to come up with their own answers.

Granted, in all fields (including ours), there is a certain amount of memorization you must do in order to have the basic knowledge to use the tools and have a starting place to make discernments. For example, in learning Greek and Hebrew, the memorization of some paradigms and vocabulary is required, and your opinion on a particular category of verbs or definition of a vocabulary word really does not matter. The same goes for learning the jargon of the field (all of those -ologies), basic events and figures in church history, and major theological concepts and positions. But simply to fill your head with assorted facts is hardly an education, though it may make you popular when picking teams to play Trivial Pursuit™, or perhaps Bible trivia in your case.

I have already encouraged you to ask questions as part of your educational process, but having done that, you must take the answers you find and subject them to disciplined, rigorous thought. This does not have to be a process for you alone, and it is preferable to work through such issues in community, including the historical church community, the scholarly community, your community of peers, and the congregational community.

Thinking in general is pretty easy, but disciplined, critical thinking is hard work. It takes time and energy to read and study widely enough on a matter to have some idea of the relevant issues and then consider and weigh all of that information to reach a conclusion. It takes concentration to get past impressive rhetoric and appealing prose to get at the heart of an argument and see if merits acceptance. It takes patience to let issues percolate in your mind and devise arguments and counterarguments, pros and cons, on the matters. It also takes a certain amount of courage to then come to a conclusion and be ready to defend it and, if need be, modify it in light of responses. This discipline of critical thinking will transfer into your ministry as those you serve ask you questions expecting a thoughtful response and then come back at you with "Yeah, well what about . . . ?"

A danger of the failure to think is that it leads you to simply accept the last idea you heard or one that strikes your fancy, without considering the merits of the idea or whether it is biblically and theologically sound. As a student, you can easily get caught up with new or seemingly radical ideas simply because they are new or radical. You become convicted because a teacher or writer is so passionate about his or her views that you get caught up in the emotion or rhetoric without actually considering the content. Thus, without actually thinking through the other options (assuming the teacher is fair to the issue and presents other options), you can end up claiming this wonderful new view as your own.

First, every such idea has to be tested. Given the Christian claim to stand under biblical authority, these ideas have to be examined first in light of Scripture. I remember a time when I was presenting to my grandfather (the one who read the Bible through multiple times a year) some new, wonderful theological idea I had picked up. I would assert, "the Bible says . . ." when, in truth, a book about the Bible had said it. He countered that the Bible did not say that—anywhere. And the more I thought about it, he was right. But it sure was a neat idea. Second, the idea also should be reflected upon in light of the church's thinking on the matter over time. In most cases, you will find that someone has presented a similar idea along the way and that idea has had its critics.[1] Hence church history and historical theology come into play. Third, examine the speakers or writers, as best you can. Do they have an axe to grind or a hobbyhorse that is rarely dismounted? What presuppositions and other baggage are behind their claims? Do they delight in novelty or controversy, or do they show

---

1. A friend of mine reminds his students that there is a word that is usually applied to the discovery of things in Scripture that no one else has ever seen. That word is "heresy."

respect for (even if disagreement with) other understandings? Fourth, consider the evidence for and against their position and the overall coherence of their position. For example, is their point really supported by the evidence they give (if any) or do they build their argument on unsubstantiated assertions or suppositions?[2]

The point is not to deny an appropriate place for persuasive rhetoric or new ideas. The point is to encourage you to think past the rhetoric and through the new ideas. Helmut Thielicke aptly summarizes the proper response to what you read or hear:

> My plea is simply this: every theological idea which makes an impression upon you must be regarded as a challenge to your faith. Do not assume as a matter of course that you believe whatever impresses you theologically or enlightens you intellectually. Otherwise suddenly you are believing no longer in Jesus Christ, but in Luther or one of your other theological teachers.[3]

Think about it.

2. A useful resource for learning to read critically, and, I think, by extension to think through arguments critically, is Mortimer Adler and Charles Van Doren's *How to Read a Book*, rev. ed. (New York: Touchstone, 1972).

3. Helmut Thielicke, *A Little Exercise for Young Theologians* (Grand Rapids: Eerdmans, 1962; reprinted 1998), 31.

10

Associate with People Who Don't Share Your Views

A NATURAL tendency when thrown into a situation where a lot of new and challenging ideas are tossed your way is to seek refuge among the like-minded. There you can dwell safely among those who will reassure you that you are right and that you need not be troubled by other opinions that could suggest your own are wrong. This is exactly what I did during much of my theological training. It was not really necessary in my first master's program, where I already agreed with much of what was said or simply took new information at face value because it fit nicely into my own understanding of things. When I moved on to a second master's degree at a seminary in another denomination, however, I found myself the exception rather than the rule. Over time, I gradually found allies among others from similar backgrounds, who were there for whatever reason. The situation is somewhat ironic because the reason one of my professors at my first school encouraged me to go to the other school was to challenge and broaden my views. By the way, my observation is that such clustering is common among students of all theological stripes.

The tragedy of such a strategy is that you can miss out on much of the challenge, growth, and fun of theological education. To associate with those who differ with you has numerous benefits for your education and beyond. First, you learn to defend your views, or whether they are worth defending at all. That is, spending time with those who differ with you forces you to think about what you believe and why you believe it. Your views might well be worthwhile, and if so, they ought to be shared. If not, perhaps it will become obvious to you. Second, you learn to have dialog rather than fights with people who disagree with you. Third, and in connection with the previous point, as you get to know these other students or teachers, you learn that intelligent, honest, sincere people can look at the same evidence and come away with different conclusions. Fourth, you can gain insight into how and why other people think as they do. You can see how their upbringing, culture, ethnicity, economic status, church background (or lack thereof), and the like affect the way they look at things. So, on the one hand, you gain sympathy, even if you are not convinced. At the same time, it might help you to recognize how much your own upbringing, culture, ethnicity, economic status, church background, and the like affect the way you look at things. Finally, and perhaps, most importantly, you make friends, or better, recognize your sisters and brothers in Christ and develop a love for them that transcends the differences (even if neither of you gives up your views).

A good route to engage other students is to get to know them outside the classroom (I would say the same for getting to know teachers). Spending time together in the dining hall, around a game table, on the softball field, or serving in the soup kitchen (perhaps especially in the soup kitchen!) will probably give you a different perspective on the other students than if you only encounter them in the classroom.

While it is possible that you will discover they are narrow-minded jerks inside and outside the classroom (or they may discover that about you!), it is more likely that you find reasons to appreciate and respect them, even if you never agree on particular issues.

Finally, engaging such people during your theological education is a good training ground for your encounters with such people in your ministry, who are far more difficult to avoid. Hashing out differences, defending your views, conceding when you need to do so, and learning to live with disagreement in seminary will hopefully equip you to do the same in your ministry.

In seminary, I usually hated group activities, because I did not want to have to listen to other people drone on about things I did not believe and because I did not want my grade dependent on them (I am not proud of either of these lines of reasoning now!). However, one teacher explained that he used groups precisely to give us practice for church. In the groups, I found people with whom I disagreed, likewise in church. Some were so self-assured and others had no convictions, likewise in church. Others really irritated me and I them, likewise in church. In these groups we had to learn to work together despite our differences, so also in church. And now, though I know some of my students hate it, I require work groups in some of my classes for the exact same reasons.

11

Speak Up without Talking Down

Two topics that almost beg for heated discussion are politics and religion, and, while you may be able to avoid the former during your theological education (though I doubt it), it is pretty hard to avoid the latter. It is also one of the areas in which people find themselves most emotionally vested, and so a negative word toward their views or opinions can be perceived as a personal attack. Add to this potentially explosive situation the competitiveness and arrogance that often accompanies academic pursuits, and heated discussions are almost a guarantee. Yet a theological education requires you to engage sensitive issues with fellow students and your instructors.

Some try to avoid the conflict by avoiding the conversations, or at least by never offering a contrary point of view. Perhaps they do so either because they do not want to cause a negative reaction in someone else—hurt feelings, anger, uncontrollable sobbing—or they do not have the confidence to assert their own views. Perhaps they do so because somewhere along the way they were taught the mistaken notion that Christians should never dispute or that Christian unity requires uniformity (or, at least, quiet surrender). However, avoidance will only work so long. If you manage to hide from such conflicts while in school, they will find you once you enter ministry work, at least if that work involves, in any way, other people. And if you think there are *no* issues worth discussing frankly and openly, and even arguing over, then you are taking your faith commitments far too lightly.

Another factor that affects what students are willing to say is institutional bias, implicit or overt, against certain points of view. Students sometimes know these taboo opinions going in, but at other times they discover them only when they have stepped on the land mine and it blows up in their face. In some schools, students are fearful of speaking lest they be labeled an "–ist" of some sort (racist, sexist, exclusivist, fundamentalist, etc.) because their views do not align with the political correctness of their institutions. I am not talking about name-calling or degrading others here, which is certainly out of place. On the other hand, other schools employ unofficial or official sanctions if a student voices unorthodox positions in the course of exploring options, or if a student questions that school's longstanding consensus on how the Gospel intersects with social issues. In either case, the spoken or unspoken limits have a chilling effect on free thought and discussion.

The reluctance to speak up can also arise because of the male-female dynamic in the classroom. I can speak with some authority to one side of the issue, but I have to rely on what my female students tell me for the other side. A man's fear of publicly challenging the opinion of a woman, that is, taking on her arguments in class, has sometimes stifled what could otherwise be helpful discussions. Some men will not challenge a woman because they have been told it is not the gentlemanly thing to do, while others do it because they have been led to think it is sexist and, perhaps, an attempt to reestablish patriarchy. Admittedly, some men don't dispute a woman's opinion because they are sexist. From what my female students have told me, however, they far prefer to have the men in the class engage and challenge their opinions than for the men to clam up, for whatever reason. On the other hand, there are still some men who will dismiss a woman's opinion simply because she is a woman, which is also sexist. To refuse to debate a woman's point of view on any of the grounds I have suggested hinders rather than helps the education of both the man and the woman because it stifles healthy, honest dialog. More importantly, such a practice indicates that the woman's point of view is not being taken seriously, and it suggests that the man is taking her faith commitments too lightly, both of which may lead her to keep quiet rather than be continually disrespected. Similar dynamics can come into play in discussions among students of differing races and ethnicities.

When dealing with classroom discussions, I have at times given my students guidelines in cases where blood pressures and tempers can rise. I use game imagery, not because I don't take the discussions seriously, but because games are carried out within a structured environment that allows for freedom that does not spin out of control.

First, come prepared to play. Here, I am primarily talking about those discussions where the class was to read or prepare in advance in some way. There are few things more irritating for students and teachers alike than to have to listen to someone reel off his or her own insights when it is clear they have not come prepared to discuss the topic at hand. They confidently assert, "I think this" and "I think that," when there is little evidence of thinking at all, at least thinking about the actual assignment. So if you did not prepare, do not participate, and accept the consequences. Don't be an impediment to the general conversation.

Second, play hard but play nice. Speak your mind, and defend your point of view. Take a chance and offer a thought that has been brewing in the back of your mind. But try not to be obnoxious. Avoid name calling or simply impugning the character of another speaker. Engage the other person's issues and arguments (after first giving them a fair hearing). So try, for example, "Here are the problems I see with what you are saying" or "Have you considered . . ." And when you are challenged, don't throw a fit or a chair. Rather, listen to what the other person has to say and think about it. You may need to defend, concede, or consider further. Keep in mind that such discussions do not have to end with the issues resolved. Of course, if the conversation is simply about how each student "feels" about a topic (as opposed to thinking about it), then there really is no place or point to engage what they have said, other than perhaps to affirm that you have heard them.

Third, everybody plays. It is hard to have a discussion when only one person is talking or when someone (often a teacher!) is manipulating the conversation toward a predetermined conclusion. The only way to get different points of view on the table is to allow people to express different points of view. So give everyone a chance to speak. Although this may be the teacher's responsibility depending on the way the discussion is set up, don't let one person dominate the discussion, and try to draw out (without humiliating) those who are less inclined to speak. By the way, if you do not think anyone is dominating the discussion, you may well ask whether you are.

Fourth, keep your head in the game. That is, stay on topic and pay attention to what is being said. Rabbits are fine to chase if you are Elmer Fudd, but in classroom discussions they tend to prevent engagement with the issue at hand and may represent a lack of preparation. And when other people are talking, listen to what they are saying and try to understand rather than formulating your brilliant rejoinder in advance. Finally, to stay focused, put away work for other classes and turn off your phone. One of my colleagues now gives a "presence grade" as opposed to simply checking attendance. That is, he expects the mind to be there with the body and engaged in the class.

All of these "rules of the game" will carry over into your ministry work. You will be expected to enter discussions prepared, instead of going off the cuff all of the time. You will have to engage people with whom you disagree and from whom you can learn. Since we already have a Lord over the church, your point of view will not and should not necessarily carry the day, so everyone involved should be invited into the conversation. And the people you will serve will notice when your mind wanders, whether you are paying attention to what they are saying, or whether you are constantly checking your phone. In class and in ministry, take others seriously by taking what they say seriously. This too models love of neighbor and the golden rule.

12

Respect Your Teachers, but Don't Idolize Them

WHEN I first began teaching, I had the disconcerting experience of teaching a second section of the same class taught by a popular and more experienced teacher, whose class met at the same time as mine and just a couple of doors down. Every day when he walked into his classroom, I heard applause and cheers. When I walked into mine at the same time, I got a few smiles and a lot of blank stares. I later discovered that the shouts and clapping were part of a running joke with this teacher and a number of students who had taken him for other classes. While that allayed my sense of inferiority a bit, it also made me realize that this teacher was very much adored and respected by his students. Certainly much of it had to do with his winning personality, wonderful dry sense of humor, and overall kind demeanor, but I am convinced that it also had to do with the fact that he is a very good teacher.

Some teachers have a special quality that draws students to them, and those students absorb what they say and echo it as the gospel truth. The power to sway students is enhanced further by those three magical letters that follow most professors' names: PhD. Many people in the church have developed some sort of immunity to these letters and, thus, they are often far less impressed. But this is, in part, why the students come to theological schools, to learn from those knowledgeable women and men who have committed themselves to the study of theology, church history, ministry, the biblical text, and other theological disciplines.

Indeed, it is right for students to respect their professors, and not simply the ones they are drawn to. These men and women have put in many years and countless hours studying and researching to prepare themselves to teach. While different motives drive them, I think most desire to teach in the theological arena because of their own passion for Christ and his church and because of a sense of calling to the ministry of scholarship and teaching. They see teaching you as a ministry. Many also have experience as pastors and teachers in the church or in other forms of ministry. Because of their study and experience they can offer you a lot, and you should give them a fair, respectful hearing. You do not have to, nor should you, accept all that any teacher says as the final word on the matter, but give them the courtesy of your attention and serious consideration of what they offer.

If you do begin to gravitate toward a certain teacher, do not do so simply because she speaks with enthusiasm and humor or because you like his style of teaching. Don't home in only on the teachers who easily jump into conversations about the playoffs or most popular TV shows and movies. Don't assume that the younger teachers or those who are of your own gender or theological leanings are better equipped to speak to you and your future as a minister. All of those things are fine in themselves, but none on their own is an indicator of a good teacher. Parker Palmer, in his *The Courage to Teach*, says that in his interviews and conversations with students about good teaching, there was no common denominator in terms of the style or technique of the teacher. Rather, when discussing their good teachers, the students in some way or another noted a certain authenticity and investment in the subject matter that shone through in the teaching. The good teachers were engaged in and believed in what they taught. Teaching their subject was not just a job but a passion.[1] The only way to find teachers like this is to give all of your teachers a chance.

Consider other factors as well. Does the teacher seem to love or despise his or her students? However, bear in mind that the teacher may not necessarily manifest love for students by being chatty, giving pats on the back, or with daily inquiries about your well-being. Some of us are a bit more introverted. Is the teacher fair with students and respectful toward them when he comments on their work? When a teacher is dealing with an issue, is she fair to various points of view, even if she thinks they are wrong or ridiculous? Does the teacher seem to be willing to learn from his students? For example, in a recent eulogy for the late biblical scholar Nahum Sarna, the author noted with affection how whenever Sarna taught a class, he would pull out note cards that contained the interpretations and insights of students on Scripture texts. Sarna had gathered these over the years and incorporated them in subsequent classes, giving credit to the former students.[2]

1. Parker J. Palmer, *The Courage to Teach* (San Francisco: Jossey-Bass, 1998), 10. I highly recommend this book to anyone entering the teaching profession in any way, including the teaching ministry in the church.

2. Marc Zvi Brettler, in a eulogy delivered at Brandeis University on June 24, 2005. Accessed at http://www.sbl-site.org/assets/pdfs/sarna.pdf on October 31, 2008.

I think three other questions are important in looking for good teachers. First, does she *demonstrate*, in some way, critical thinking as she teaches? Can you see the teacher working through a problem in the class when one is raised, weighing the options and justifying a position? Second, is he humble enough to admit he does not have all of the answers or even that he is wrong? Third, does she practice what she preaches? That is, if she continually raises in class the need to serve the poor or to care for the elderly of the church, is she actually doing something herself in these areas? This is not to belittle the importance of raising awareness as a part of addressing problems, nor does it mean a teacher should put her acts of righteousness on display. But part of authenticity, it seems to me, is being convicted enough to act upon what we declare to a class is important.

But again, do not idolize or hang your faith on any teacher. Every teacher is human and so carries the potential—indeed the likelihood!—to be wrong, to fail, and to disappoint you. Teachers are at best imperfect channels or vessels for the teaching that will aid you in your ministry.

Finally, even if a teacher exhibits none of these good qualities I have mentioned here and their classes are bone dry but required, remember that with respectful attention you might just come across pearls of wisdom and insight that you would not have found otherwise. And remember, as I am sure my own students will attest, if God can speak through Balaam's ass (Numbers 22:28–30), he can speak through any teacher. That will be good for you to remember as well if you stand before a congregation one day!

13

Own Your Faith

ONE DAY the president of a major seminary walked into the chapel and found a young man sitting in one of the pews weeping. "What's the matter?" he asked. The student replied, "I don't know what to believe any more. Since I have been here everything I was certain about has been turned upside down." To which the president replied, "Good. That's what is supposed to happen in seminary." He then explained to the student that a process of breaking down precedes the process of rebuilding and strengthening a student's theological convictions.

Can he be serious? Isn't the point of seminary to reinforce faith? Well, yes and no. Certainly the point is not to destroy faith, at least faith worth having. Instead of simply reinforcing faith, however, the goal is more to examine and build your faith. In part, a theological education should help you move from an inherited and unexamined faith to an owned faith.[1] A seminary education that simply reaffirms what you already believe might be comforting, but is it really an education? A seminary education that simply tells you what to think and

1. This is what Howard W. Stone and James O. Duke call moving from an "embedded theology" to a "deliberative theology" in their very helpful little book, *How to Think Theologically*, 2nd ed.(Fortress Press, 2006).

believe is better termed indoctrination. What's more, to examine and question one's faith is not being unfaithful. It is seeking to be *more* faithful to God's revelation of himself in Jesus Christ as recorded in Scripture and lived out in the history of the church, past and present.

The problem with examining your faith is that it does turn things upside down for a while (sometimes a long while) and can make you think you are being untrue and unappreciative to all that you received from your parents, grandparents, pastors, and Sunday school teachers. To be certain, some have suggested directly or indirectly that theological education is dangerous for the very reason that it holds up precious beliefs to scrutiny. I heard about one preacher who beseeched a seminary faculty to stop teaching students to think outside the box so much and help them think inside the box. My response, in part, would have been, "I would at least like them to think *about* the box." To examine your faith does not diminish the wonderful and valuable things passed on from others. Instead it takes those things seriously as matters of such importance that they deserve careful thought both in terms of content and in terms of how those truths received might better be enacted in the present day.

I have observed firsthand the difficult and painful trek from an inherited faith to an owned faith, both in my students and in myself. When you have been taught all your life and have built your faith on a certain view of the Bible and the church, but then your own examination of these matters leads you to think otherwise, it can feel like not only your views on particular issues but your whole faith is crumbling. It is as though the supports to your faith are being kicked out one by one, so that the whole structure may soon come crashing down. I have seen some of my students brought to tears and others brought to a fear of how their parents or churches will respond if it is discovered that they no longer believe as they always have. The situation is intensified when different teachers are offering contradicting, but equally plausible, points of view on the same issues.

I have been there too, when I did not know what to believe and was afraid everything I thought was true was slipping away. Psychologists call this experience of confusion *cognitive dissonance*,[2] which suggests that we invest ourselves in beliefs or views that, to us, are obvious and rational. When something challenges these beliefs, especially ones that are foundational to our larger thinking or understanding, we may find it upsetting or jarring (i.e., it creates dissonance). We then seek strategies to deal with what is shaking our world. A first step might simply be to stay away from things that create such problems. In a seminary context, we may avoid teachers, classes, and other students who are likely to rock our boat. If the problem cannot simply be avoided, we may take a second step of seeking the company of those who think like us. Thus, in our theological education, we find like-minded students and teachers who assure us we are right and everyone else is wrong, fooled, dishonest, or crazy. If need be, a third tactic can be redefining the issues or explaining our way around the problems in order to convince ourselves what appears to be a problem is not really one at all. It may in fact be that the con-

2. The theory of cognitive dissonance was developed by Leon Festinger. My introduction to the theory came from and my understanding of it is filtered through Robert P. Carroll's *When Prophecy Failed: Cognitive Dissonance in the Prophetic Traditions of the Old Testament* (New York: Seabury, 1979).

flict between our view and the new information is perceived rather than real. However, sometimes the drive to maintain our particular view can lead us to treat the evidence selectively or unfairly (though we may not do so consciously). Finally, if all else fails or if we recognize our view simply will not hold up, we may have to change our minds and sort through the rubble, seeking to rebuild.

Admittedly, some never get past the first step because it hurts too much or too much is lost. They retreat into a safe but unexamined faith. The problem is that if the issues are not confronted during one's education, they will probably come up in the course of one's ministry. It seems to me that if students are going to have a crisis in moving from an inherited to owned faith, better to do it in seminary, where there are faculty and other students who have been through the same process or are going through it now. Better to experience the crisis in a place where they can find sympathy and support than to have a breakdown in the midst of their ministry, so that when confronted with the issues they cry out, "My God, I never thought about that! What am I going to do?" Again, the whole process may be painful and scary, but it is not uncommon. Hear this again: *It is not uncommon.* You are not the only theological student to experience it.

Let me be clear: I am not suggesting that you will have to abandon all you believe. Indeed, you may return to many of your original understandings. Rather, I am suggesting that seminary is the place where you will examine your faith commitments and those of others and in the process come to own your faith. I am also not suggesting that you must go through it alone—just the opposite. Your theological schooling, along with a healthy church life, provides a safer environment for you to make the move from an inherited to an owned faith. The theological breaking down and rebuilding process that so often occurs is something akin to the process of getting physically stronger. Muscle has to be broken down through exercise before it can be rebuilt even stronger than it was before, and often pain is associated with that process. Confidence about some things will return over time, though growing in your faith understanding should remain an ongoing, lifelong process. When you stop growing, you can become stagnant, ossified, and eventually die. The same is true when your faith stops growing.

PART TWO

Finding Your Way Spiritually

14

Maintain a Strong Devotional Life

O NE OF the unfortunate outcomes for many theological students during their education is that God becomes more and more an object of study and less and less the Lord with whom they are in relationship. Theological study ceases to become formation for ministry or, to again cite Anselm, "faith seeking understanding." Instead the goal becomes simply the mastery of subject matter, with God as one of or perhaps the chief subject. Along these lines, Thielicke offers the following warning:

> The man who studies theology, and especially he who studies dogmatics, might watch carefully whether he increasingly does not think in the third rather than in the second person. You know what I mean by that. This transition from one to the other level of thought, from a personal relationship with God to a merely technical reference, usually is exactly synchronized with the moment that I can no longer read the word of Holy Scripture as a word to me, but only as the object of exegetical endeavors. This is the first step towards the worst and most widespread ministers' disease.[1]

1. Thielicke, *A Little Exercise for Young Theologians*, 33. The lack of gender inclusive language is reflective of the time in which Thielicke wrote.

In addition, theological students often find themselves overwhelmed by the amount of work they have to do, so the nurturing of their relationship with God gets pushed to the backburner as they pursue their studies about God and ministry. Thus, as they leave school to serve in a ministry, they find themselves talking about a God who has become something of a stranger to them over the last few years.

As I have already discussed, by its very nature theological study can and often does upset a student's original faith construct. Questions are raised and satisfactory answers are slow in coming, if they ever do. This situation, in itself, is not necessarily a bad thing. However, it can create barriers between students and God as they discover that all they thought they knew about God may not actually be the case. I remember walking back to my dorm room one day after wrestling through some issue my seminary studies had raised, and I began quietly singing the hymn based on 2 Timothy 1:12: "I know whom I have believed and am persuaded that he is able to keep that which I have committed unto him against that day."[2] On this particular day, the thought in this verse expressed the only thing of which I felt sure. I still believed, but it was becoming more difficult to define much of what I believed with certainty.

For these reasons, my suggestion is that you develop a strong, disciplined devotional life to help you maintain your relationship with the living and loving God (as, perhaps, opposed to the textbook God) and to sustain you in those periods of frustration and doubt. When I was in seminary, students began to ask for courses in spiritual formation,

2. The hymn is Daniel W. Whittle's "I Know Whom I Have Believed" (1883).

revealing their hunger for the presence of God with them as they trod the frequently barren wilderness of their theological study. I see the same longings in my own students, and it is little wonder that one of the most popular classes among our students is "Spiritual Formation for Ministry."

The structure of your devotional life may differ from that of others, but I would recommend the regular practice of at least four disciplines. What follows is admittedly cursory. I could say much more on each of the disciplines that I discuss below, and there are many others that you could include. Indeed, I encourage you to read more on the disciplines to better understand the practices and their purposes.[3] But to my mind and in my experience, these are basic and primary means for maintaining a relationship with God that will help you weather the storms of theological study.

First, set aside a time or times for prayer daily. Prayers on the fly are fine, but regular periods of conversation with and submission to God in prayer are essential to sustaining a healthy spiritual life. Pray even when you do not feel like it or are uncertain that God is listening. Use written prayers,[4] biblical prayers, spontaneous prayers, whichever you find most conducive to your speaking with God. Offer praise to God.

3. An excellent, accessible, concise resource for the theology and practice of the spiritual disciplines is Gary Holloway and Earl Lavender, *Living God's Love: An Invitation to Christian Spirituality* (Abilene, TX: Leafwood, 2004). For a more detailed discussion of various individual disciplines see Richard J. Foster, *Celebration of Discipline*, rev. ed. (San Francisco: Harper San Francisco, 1988). A more popular-level but very helpful treatment of spiritual disciplines is John Ortberg's *The Life You've Always Wanted* (Grand Rapids: Zondervan, 1997).

4. See, for example, Phyllis Tickle's *The Divine Hours* series published by Doubleday.

Pray for your own submission to the will of God, to have daily needs met, for forgiveness and the ability to forgive, and for preservation from evil (sound familiar?). Lay your needs and requests before God, but also offer your thanksgiving. The goal is not to make yourself feel "spiritual" but to allow God to make you Spirit-filled by conforming you life and your will to his.

Second, read and meditate on Scripture. Do not read in preparation for classes or lessons or to solve some theological problem. Read to hear God speaking to you. Some find it helpful to keep a record of thoughts on their reading in a private journal, not to list supposedly profound insights but simply to record what they are hearing in Scripture. Also, read prayerfully. Ask for God to speak to you through your reading. Allow the words of Scripture to evoke and shape prayers as you hear God's word. End with a prayer asking for the will to submit to God's word.

Third, participate in the worship and life of a church on a committed, regular basis. There is no Christianity apart from the church, and a Christian who refuses the fellowship of the church cuts himself or herself off from the life-giving body of Christ. In the church's worship, God encounters us and in that encounter blesses and sustains us. In the church's fellowship, one finds the love of Christ through the love of Christian sisters and brothers, a love that is especially important for a struggling seminarian. Additionally, the church reminds theological students why they are pursing their education.[5]

Fourth, find ways to serve in the name of Christ, particularly service to those who are poor and in need. It is in service

5. Involvement in the life of the church is further discussed in the next chapter.

that you express the love of Christ to others (John 13:13–16), and glorify God before others (Matthew 5:13–16), and you encounter Christ in those served (Matthew 25:31–40). In Christian service, you are reminded whom you serve and why you serve, and you encounter him in that service.

These disciplines, along with others that you incorporate in your spiritual life, will draw you closer to God and open you to his work in your life as you go through your studies. They will also ingrain spiritual habits that will continue to bless and strengthen you through the ups and downs of ministry and of life.

15

Go to Church

Iᴋɴᴏᴡ of one seminary where the students annually gave a mock award called the "Boxspring Presbyterian Award." It is given to the student who most consistently slept in on Sunday mornings. No doubt students could compete for a similar award at many if not most seminaries. While the award itself is intended to be humorous, I think it reveals an alarming problem that is not confined to that one seminary: Many theological students do not participate in a local church during their years in school.

If I am ever on a minister search committee and we are considering someone straight out of seminary, here are two questions I will ask. First, where did you go to church during seminary and for how long? Second, what was your role or ministry in that church? That is, were you active in the church's life? My concern is that if the candidate did not invest himself or herself in a local congregation for that two or three years, then why would I trust that person to teach me, my children, or my church about what it means to be a part of the community of God? Can I trust them to be committed to our church over the long-term since they will have avoided the most concrete expression of Kingdom life throughout their theological training?

How is it that those who plan to spend their lives in service to the church can spend two, three, or more years without actually committing themselves to a local church? Do they see it as their last chance to be free of the boredom and monotony of regular involvement in a church before they are paid to contribute to that boredom and monotony? Do they see the church as unimportant in their own spiritual development? Is church fine, as long as one is paid to go?

Participation in a particular, local church is an essential element of theological education for a number of reasons, the most important of which is the biblical one. There is no Christianity, no membership in the body of Christ, apart from participation in an assembly of believers. The Bible's language of being a member of the body of Christ has nothing to do with choosing to join a group as one would join a civic club or wholesale warehouse club. When Paul talks about membership in the body, he uses an image of actual body parts: foot, hand, ear, eye, nose, and head (see 1 Corinthians 12). These are organic parts of a whole, as are we who belong to a local church. Any of these members severed from the body will die, and the body itself will suffer.

Another reason that participation in a local church is vital for someone preparing for church ministry is that there you find the kind of people you will serve after graduation. Strangely enough, one finds church folk in churches, not in books about churches. So church becomes the place where the abstract and theoretical lessons of the classroom encounter the flesh and blood realities of church life. The marvelous thing about most church bodies is that they will not allow you to keep things at merely an abstract and theoretical level. They want to know what your classroom learning has to do with their Christian walk in the boardroom, high school classroom, living room, hospital waiting room, and locker room. When you fully participate in the life of a local church, you have a practical training ground to begin moving your learning from your head to your hands, feet, and knees, as you serve fellow members.

Regular participation in a local church also teaches you to love the church. More about this will be said in chapter 18, but let it suffice for the moment to say that it is an easy thing to love the church in theory. When real faces, attitudes, annoying quirks, and outright jerks are sitting next to you week in and week out, the decision to love becomes concrete. You have to learn to deal with these people in a loving way, just as you will when you are called to a church or ministry after graduation.

Going to the same church on an ongoing basis also reinforces your understanding of commitment and covenant, both of which have fallen on hard times lately. Just as it is far easier to flit from relationship to relationship or from friendship to friendship, seeking what satisfies me most, it is much easier to jump from church to church or only hang about the periphery than it is to invest myself fully. As in a marriage or in a friendship, investing ourselves fully in a church opens us to the possibility both of great joy and great pain. It disciplines us to work through issues and seek what is best for the body as a whole, rather than for ourselves. It teaches us to deal with issues that will inevitably come up in whatever church you covenant yourself to as a minister or member. How we engage in and live out these kinds of human covenants is surely reflective of how we engage in and live out our covenant with

Jesus Christ, a covenant which also promises both suffering and joy.

Finally, being a part of a local church will provide you with the spiritual support that you will need in your daily walk with Christ, and especially as your theological studies challenge your spiritual and emotional stability. The point here is not, "What's in it for me at this church?" However, we were made for community with fellow Christians, and in that community we not only offer service and support, we are served and supported. This is a blessing of the body of Christ, and it is not to be missed.

16

Find a Mentor

GIVEN THE current arrangement we find in most churches, where churches are segregated along age lines, and if large enough, the age groups may never encounter each other except in the lobby or the bathroom, I am afraid that many young people miss out on one of God's greatest gifts in the church: relationships with fellow Christians who have long experienced walking with Jesus. Perhaps because we tend to associate with those who are in the same age range or life situation, we cut ourselves off (intentionally or not) from the wisdom of those who can help us discern direction and significance in our spiritual lives. Such guidance can be especially helpful for theological students precisely because they are so often young (usually twenty-somethings) and do not yet know how to correlate what they are getting in the classroom with what is going on in the church. Or their own spiritual development, whatever their age, has yet to catch up with their intellectual development. Thielicke describes such a student: "There is a hiatus between the area of the young theologian's actual spiritual growth and what he already knows intellectually about this arena."[1]

1. Thielicke, *Little Exercise for Young Theologians*, 10 (italics original). In this light, Thielicke makes an analogy between the theological student and a boy given oversized pants that he must grow into. Thielicke

A spiritual mentor, one who has long walked the path of discipleship, becomes a valuable means for the student to begin closing that gap. A mentor is not someone who simply dispenses unconnected bits of wisdom. The mentor helps the student integrate all aspects of life, including theological studies, into her or his Christian walk. He or she is more of a guide, who knows the paths and pitfalls of the spiritual life that the student is encountering, will encounter, or may encounter.

How do you find a mentor? Some schools have mentoring programs in place where students are assigned to faculty mentors or area pastors. You may thrive in such an arrangement and if your school does it, give it a chance. However, I have personally found such arrangements somewhat artificial and difficult. It seems to me that voluntary mentoring relationships are more productive. In addition, unless the faculty member is also clearly heavily invested in the life of the church, regularly participating in the worship, fellowship, and service life of the church, you may find that he or she is not especially well-suited to help you bridge the gap between intellectual and spiritual development. If there is such a faculty member who is willing to enter into such a relationship with you, great! Otherwise, your best bet is to look within your church.

You will know the person by his or her fruit. That is, the one you want to mentor you should be one who is obviously Spirit-led, devoted to Christ and his church, and who regularly shows love for others. She or he should also have

---

later describes this state as "theological puberty" (p. 12). He takes his discussion in a different direction than I do, but his description suits my purposes here.

a reputation for spiritual wisdom, knowing how to connect experience and knowledge to the spiritual life, which is different than someone who is simply intellectually gifted. He or she should also be more experienced than you, having had enough time to have the experiences and develop the wisdom that will be helpful to share with you. Ask around. Those who have been in your church a while can point out such people to you.

While the mentor does not have to be a pastor or minister, such a person may offer the advantage of knowing what you are going through in your education and what you will face after graduation. It should at least be someone who respects theological education. I know of some theological students at one church who could have benefited greatly from the wisdom and experience of one of the ministers who had been there for many years. However, the minister's own bad experience with theological education (and perhaps his bad experiences with know-it-all theological students) caused him, before members of his church, to deride repeatedly the institution where these students went. Instead of the seminary, he referred to the school as the "theological cemetery, where they bury the truth." He actually had a lot of good things to teach these students, which hopefully they availed themselves of, but he was not a good choice as a mentor simply because he seemed to have so little respect for what those students were doing.

It is also a good idea to choose a mentor of the same gender. While men can certainly learn from women and women from men in mentoring relationships, there are certain things about each other that we do not get—the whole Venus and Mars thing. Also, since these mentoring relationships can become deeply personal, there could be a danger of a physical relationship growing out of the mentoring relationship. Thus, to avoid such complications, I think it is best for the mentor and student to be the same gender.

Once you identify someone you think would make a good mentor, perhaps someone already mentoring others, approach her or him about the opportunity. If this person agrees, then you have to define the relationship in some way. Regular meeting times are preferable, whatever the mentor's and your schedules can accommodate. Meeting in person is better than over the phone or through e-mail because relationships are better developed face-to-face. However, these other means can have a place if either of you are especially busy or when you are eventually separated after graduation. In your meetings, pray together and be intentional about discussing issues relating to your spiritual growth. If the situation allows, you may also find opportunities to accompany your mentor in order to see him or her in acts of Christian service.

Finally, the mentoring relationship is not one of peers because you have chosen to go to this person for her/his wisdom, experience, and ability to help guide you. While a certain amount of openness in both directions may occur, the mentor will not necessarily see you as a confidant or best friend and need not do so. You are with this person to learn and be led, to find a model to emulate. Thus, the mentor is unlikely to become your buddy, though often a relationship will grow that you will treasure for a lifetime.

I have actually enjoyed the guidance of several mentors— men who have led, counseled, and walked with me in the ups and downs of ministry and of life in general—throughout my theological education and to this very day. For example, when

I began my theological education, the preaching minister at the church where I served as a campus minister quickly became a mentor to me. Jerrie is a devout, reflective, plain-spoken man who generously shared his time, experience, and wisdom with me. When I ran into roadblocks, he helped me see how to get around them, through them, or live with them. But he also modeled for me, in his ministry and personal life, deep spiritual devotion, integrity, and seriousness, as well as humor. When I conducted my first funeral, he was the one I went to for guidance, and likewise when I performed my first wedding ceremony. He continues to give of himself in this way. A couple of my own graduate students have told me how he became a mentor to them as well. This is the kind of mentor you want to find.

17

Participate in a Covenant Group

SOMEWHERE ALONG the way, many of us developed an unhealthy idea that no one else should know what messes
we can be. We think we have to carry our burdens on our
own, secretly, lest anyone find out we are (gasp!) weak sometimes. We muddle through our studies thinking we are the
only ones who are confused, upset, doubting, or just plain
lost. Sometimes, believing we are called to ministry, we feel
unsure of the specifics, and so anxiety creeps in about what
will happen after graduation.

We were never intended to carry these burdens alone.
Of course God helps us with our burdens, but I am convinced that we overlook or neglect one of God's primary
means of doing so: community. Fellow Christians are one
of the ways that God encourages us and helps us. They are
also one of the ways God sets us straight and tells us what
we need to hear, even if we do not want to hear it. Note the
following Bible verses:

> Carry each other's burdens, and in this way you
> will fulfill the law of Christ. (Galatians 6:2)

And we urge you, brothers and sisters, warn those who are idle and disruptive, encourage the disheartened, help the weak, be patient with everyone. (1 Thessalonians 5:14)

But encourage one another daily, as long as it is called "Today," so that none of you may be hardened by sin's deceitfulness. (Hebrews 3:13)

And let us consider how we may spur one another on toward love and good deeds, not giving up meeting together, as some are in the habit of doing, but encouraging one another—and all the more as you see the Day approaching. (Hebrews 10:24–25)

While the church body as a whole is called upon to provide such support and encouragement, many find it helpful to have a smaller group of fellow Christians who share similar circumstances as means of support and encouragement. As theological students, your questions and struggles are probably unique compared to those of the church as a whole, and there may be certain issues that those not in your shoes just would not understand. Indeed, your own struggles may raise unnecessary doubts and questions among those who are not sharing your current experiences. This is where a covenant group comes in.

I struggle for an appropriately descriptive name for the kind of group I have in mind. Some call them prayer groups or discernment groups or accountability groups. Elements of prayer, discernment, and accountability are all included, but I use "covenant groups" because it describes the nature of the relationship within the group. "Commitment groups" may work as well. It is a small group of Christians who commit or covenant to share, support, encourage, hold accountable, and pray for one another. The important thing is not what it is called but what goes on when you are together. Such a group is not, by the way, a substitute for participation in a local church; neither is it a Christian clique for the super-spiritual. Rather, it is a means of spiritual development within the Christian community that accomplishes things that are more difficult to achieve in the larger body. However, if it detracts from your love for or participation in the larger church body, you should rethink what you are doing because, in the long run, separating yourself from or looking down on the larger community will undermine your spiritual growth.

The group should be small, probably three to five members. More than two allows for differing perspectives, but over five may cause your time together to go on too long. There needs to be adequate time for sharing, confessing, discussion, and prayer, and too many people prevent that. A smaller group also facilitates intimacy and, hopefully, better ensures confidentiality. While the kind of intimacy required for frank confession and accountability may take time to develop, you should see yourself eventually being able to open up to the people you choose to join with in such a group. You must also have complete mutual trust; otherwise, the group will never likely delve below the surface-level. Artificially forming groups and throwing people into them is not likely to be helpful. All of this suggests that you may not be able to form such a group until you have been at the school and/or church long enough to see who might fit well in such a group with you. All of the group members should be the same gender as well. Believe it or not, there are struggles and issues unique to each gender.

Once you form the group, you will want to lay down some rules or guidelines to which everyone in the group commits. Some guidelines to consider and ones my own group has found helpful are the following. First, what is said in the group stays in the group. Absolute confidentiality is a must. We do not share what is said even with our wives and certainly we do not pull sermon or lesson illustrations out of the group (for example, "I know a guy, who shall remain anonymous, who told me he really struggles with . . ."). I have heard teachers and preachers treat confidential conversations this way—Christians in casual conversations too—and it made me certain that I would never open up to them. Second, we schedule a regular meeting time and try to stick to it, even if one of us has cannot come. We usually need between forty-five minutes and an hour. Third, we have a regular meeting place that is isolated enough to prevent anyone else from overhearing what is said. Thus, we have ruled out places like restaurants or the student union. Fourth, we use our time intentionally. We have some small talk but try to quickly focus on the purposes of the group: sharing, confession, encouragement, support, prayer, discernment. Fifth, no one is forced to speak at any given meeting. Sometimes one of us may have nothing to say or may need time to get the courage up to share something. Sixth, we commit to being honest with each other. No one has to share everything, but what we do share should be truthful. Likewise, our responses to the person sharing have to be honest. We are tempted sometimes to not say what needs to be said to spare someone's feelings, but such an approach will not help much in this case. One can be gentle but also forthright and say what needs to be said. Seventh, no one of us dominates the conversation, particularly in responding to what someone else has said. Finally, we commit to praying for each other and our issues until we meet again.

With respect to how you actually conduct time in your own group, you will have to see what works for everyone. It may change over time. I offer what my group does simply as an example. We begin in silence and silent prayer, centering our thoughts on God and asking him to be present among us. When someone in the group is ready to speak, he does so, though no one is forced to speak. That person may confess struggles with sin, talk about problems in his life, share good news, talk about places he has seen God at work in the last week, or seek advice. It varies from person to person and week to week. After that person has spoken, we again spend time in silence, considering what was said, praying, and listening for a word from God. We then respond to the person who has spoken, if we have anything to say. Sometimes we give suggestions, but often we ask questions to help the person clarify what God may be doing or leading him to. The goal is not to fix a problem but to facilitate spiritual discernment. At other times we simply offer praise to God or words of support and encouragement to the one who shared. We continue this process until everyone who wants to share has. We then end in a period of silent prayer, and someone usually voices a prayer at the very end to conclude our time together.

My personal testimony regarding covenant groups is that I have found it invaluable in my Christian walk. The men I meet with have helped me see God at work in new ways, helped me weather storms in my professional and personal life, and helped me discern God's will at difficult crossroads. I am closer to them and they know me more intimately than anyone else, except my wife. To my loss, I did not participate in such a group in my theological education. It could have benefited my spiritual walk during that time in so many ways. Now that I have experienced the blessing of such a group, I would not trade the experience for anything.

PART THREE

Finding Your Way in the Church

18

Love the Church

ASTRANGE thing sometimes happens to those who pursue an education that is supposed to help them serve the church. Somewhere along the way, they fall out of love with the very church they feel called to serve. They would say they love the church, but what they mean is some abstract notion of the church divorced from the realities of specific churches in specific times and places. Or, they love the ideal church, which, of course, exists only in their minds.

This is the reason people often have trouble in relationships, right? A woman formulates in her mind the ideal man, perhaps shaped by television, movies, and pop songs. She wants Superman, only one who is more attentive to his partner than Superman was to Lois Lane. Or, on a more "spiritual" level, an image shaped by what she believes the Bible teaches a man ought to be—perhaps Jesus, but without the celibacy. Or a man pictures the perfect woman, a blend of his mother (she cooks, cleans, treats him like he is the only one who matters), magazine images, and, again to be spiritual, the "wife of noble character" in Proverbs 31. He wants Wonder Woman, only a more domesticated version and without the golden lasso that compels him to tell the truth. Since no one can live up to these images and since notions of love and romance in popular culture encourage them not to "settle," they hop from relationship to relationship in love with an ideal but never a real person.

Transfer that way of thinking to a theology student's relationship with the church. She reads book after book that point out what the church "ought to be" and the stories of great reformers who changed the church. She begins to fancy herself as a reformer-in-the-making. He hears lectures on ecclesiology while also reading the latest ministry magazines in the library. From that, he develops a clear sense of what church should be and expects to actually find it out there somewhere, and if not find it, build it. These students are after a loving church, where everyone is devoted to the students' own understanding of the Bible, worship, fellowship, and service. Then they go into the church down the street and they find people who are "backwards" in their view of the Bible, whose worship they think is dated and stale, whose fellowship largely consists of banal conversation in the lobby about the weather and sports, and whose great evangelistic outreach is a poorly done and poorly attended Vacation Bible School each summer. Since they cannot love such a "dead" church, the students move a block over to the "contemporary" church only to find that the upbeat worship is really all it has going for it, since the people rarely talk to each other, service consists of giving money to projects, and whose leadership, in the end, is not really post-anything. And so our students move once more.

Thus, while such students may claim to love the church, they in fact love a fiction. Something that nowhere, at no time, has ever existed. They forget that the church is made up of fallen and fallible people like themselves. Those in the church are there for a variety of motivations, and they rarely get it "right" enough to satisfy every critic, much less one with the extensive wisdom that surely must come from one to three years of theological education.

Again and again, Scripture emphasizes that love has far less to do with what we say than what we do. It is one thing to say we love the people with whom we gather each Sunday, but it is another thing to demonstrate that love with a persistent service to them and a dedication that means we stick with them through thick and thin.

Like love for a spouse or love for our children, love for a church is forged in the day in and day out living with these people. It comes from putting up with their faults (as they put up with ours) and forgiving their offenses (as they forgive ours) over the long haul. It is easy to profess love when things are sunshine and roses, it is difficult to show love when it is storms and thorns. Just as good parents do not love their children only when they are well-behaved, attentive, and live up to the parents' dreams for them, so we love the church whether it meets all of our hopes, dreams, and expectations or not. There is a place for loving critique—as parents correct their children—but only one who has fully invested himself or herself in the life of the church and has demonstrated love for the body of Christ has the right to offer any critiques of the church.[1]

We love the church because God loves the church, the body of Christ. Indeed we will do well to remember that the

1. Admittedly, the analogy is limited, focusing on unconditional, familial love for the church. In terms of the general relationship, seminary students ought to consider themselves the children, rather than the parents, in the church.

church has a Father, who loves it in the way I have described, despite its flaws and failings. We love the church because there we are loved and learn to love—not the easy, what-is-in-it-for-me love, but the love born of giving and sacrifice to another, the kind of love Christ showed for us on the cross. We love the church because in doing so we bear witness through what we do to the self-giving love of the Lord we confess.

19

Be Humble

A GREAT tragedy of working toward a degree like a master of divinity is that students actually believe or act as though they are "masters of the divine." Something sinister about theological education is that it can create a conceit that leads the student to believe she or he has an inside track on knowing God. A little Greek and Hebrew, a smattering of theological concepts, being able to define words like "orthopraxy" and "hermeneutics," and all of the sudden a once humble student who was originally pursing a theological education to serve the church becomes a terror to the very church he or she wants to serve. No longer is the education primarily about formation and service, though that might be in the back of the student's mind somewhere. Now it is about showing off what one knows and putting in their place those who, in their darkened ignorance, do not agree with the enlightened student.

I know this to be the case because I was that student. It all started before I officially began my theological studies. Someone gave me a book on interpreting the Bible that taught me about "hermeneutics" and "exegesis," two words I began to drop into conversations. I believed that book gave me *the* key to unlocking *the* meaning of Scripture, and so I was naturally now in a position to direct the feeble minds of those in my home church. Strangely enough, most were not impressed with my two new words or my intelligence. It seems that they had been reading the Bible for ten, twenty, even fifty years longer than I had and knew a bit more than I imagined.

It became worse once I entered my first masters program and had actual classes in biblical interpretation (where we talked about hermeneutics and exegesis!), theology, church history, and biblical languages. Now I could plumb beneath the surface of my English Bible into the original languages, uncovering profound theological concepts, and really show church people the way by speaking actual Greek and Hebrew words (despite my Hebrew professor's admonition that using Greek and Hebrew words in church was just showing off). I became a terror to Sunday school teachers and preachers. They would speak and I would rebut, or at the very least give those learned, disapproving head shakes that told them they had said something wrong. It got to the point that the preacher or teacher was often checking my expression out of the corner of his or her eye, mostly to be able to duck for cover when I launched my counter-offensive. If I could not set the teacher straight during class, there was always time after class, where I could pull him off to the side and gently show him the error of his ways. It took a loving friend, who often preached and taught at our church, to point out to me that I was being a jerk (though he was too kind to use that word). In my head I was justifying it as teaching "the truth," but in reality, it was a prideful display—of what was actually my lack of love, wisdom, and knowledge.

It has since dawned on me that there is a good reason why many in churches are suspicious of those with theological education: their experience of those with theological education. I hope I was not typical, but if I was, I can understand why some church members would prefer a preacher straight out of high school to one with a seminary education. This is not to belittle the importance of theological education. It is to belittle the self-importance that can come with this education. If theological education becomes a basis for pride and an uncharitable spirit toward the church, then it does more harm than good.

I will admit that we who teach can share some of the blame in creating such students. I fear that too often in our teaching we belittle (at times ridicule), even if indirectly, those in the pew because we think they really just do not "get it." We tell the stories of bad preaching—and there is bad preaching—not simply to help our students in their tasks but to get a laugh at someone else's expense and to enhance our own sense of intellectual and theological superiority. Some of us act as if those who do not use our scholarly methods of interpretation surely cannot hear God's word properly, forgetting that people heard God's word in Scripture centuries before the development of our methods.[1] So we clone ourselves and our despicable pride in our students.

The solution is humble recognition that God has called you and me to *one* ministry in the church, a ministry that requires special preparation to be sure. The church will look to you as their guide and teacher in Scripture and theology. But you are *one* voice in the congregation's discernment of God's

---

1. I do not intend to dismiss the value of these interpretative methods so much as to relativize them to some extent by putting them into perspective. The methods are helpful for hearing the messages of Scripture, but they are historically and culturally conditioned approaches that do not have a monopoly on hearing the text.

will for the life of the body. As you help the church understand the possible meanings of Scripture (yes, I said "possible meanings") and how they bear on the life of the church, you do so lovingly and in humility, recognizing that the body is made up of many parts, and you are only one of those parts. You might consider yourself the brain, but depending on how you carry out your ministry, others in the church might move you about halfway down and on the backside.

Humility also means that you recognize that you can learn from your church. After all, there are people there who have been reading the Bible and thinking about the life of the church ten, twenty, even fifty years longer than you. Once I started listening to others, at church and in the classroom, I discovered how much I could learn from them. I have started taking notes on what my students say, and their insights join the insights of scholarly commentators the next time I teach the class. My training helps me suggest that certain interpretations may or may not legitimately arise from a given text, but their years of reading and thinking about Scripture often tell me that I need to go back and think through my interpretations again.

Humility reminds us that we are on a journey with our churches, learning and living out our faith as we go. And, unlike pride, humility allows us to walk with our churches in living out God's mission for the church.

20

Speak Boldly and Confidently

Aᶠᵗᵉʳ I took my first graduate classes in exegesis and theology, a remarkable thing happened: I became both cocky and petrified. I became cocky because now, in my mind, I had *the* key to unlock *the* truth of any biblical text, but I also often found myself frozen, afraid to teach or preach because I may have missed *the* meaning. I indicated in the previous chapter the need for theological students to exercise humility, so here I want to concentrate on the latter problem. Again, the issue for me was that if good exegesis revealed *the* original meaning of the text so that I could then move to *the* meaning for today, what if I did not get *the* meaning right?

I came to believe that every text had one original meaning, intended by the author, and that good exegesis could uncover this meaning and from there it I could easily move into the meaning for us. But problems arose for me when I went to the commentaries and other resources and discovered that the scholars themselves often did not agree on one, original meaning (among those who even buy the concept of a discoverable original meaning). Looking at the same text, they often came up with divergent, even incompatible, interpretations. They also did not agree on what the text means for today. Thus, while I became an active critic of other people's interpretations (usually some unfortunate preacher or Sunday school teacher), I often had little constructive to say because I could not with confidence assert the "right" meaning.

To complicate matters for me further, I thought that learning the biblical languages would help me to nail down more definitively that elusive single meaning of the text. I think a number of students still have this notion, and I have had one student essentially say that knowing Greek and Hebrew allows interpreters to clear up all of the ambiguity (she had not yet taken either language). A problem is that what seems clear in modern translations is often far more ambiguous in the original, and what is ambiguous in translations to begin with is not often clarified by knowing the original. I discovered that the individual Greek and Hebrew words often have several more connotations and denotations than reading the English text would suggest. Then I learned, for example, that Hebrew did not always have vowels and a change of the vowels on a word can change the meaning of a word. What's more, the critical editions of the Greek New Testament and Hebrew (and Greek!) Old Testament have those pesky notes listing variant readings (even copies of the original language texts often do not agree). Thus, I learned reading in the original languages can clear up some matters, but it can make other matters worse.[1] What was a young exegete to do with all this?

---

1. For a good defense of knowing the original languages, see Ellen F. Davis's comments in her "Teaching the Bible Confessionally in the Church," in *The Art of Reading Scripture*, ed. Ellen F. Davis and Richard B. Hays (Grand Rapids: Eerdmans, 2003), 14–15. Among the reasons she gives for studying these languages are: (1) it helps the readers recognize the "literary complexity" of the biblical text; (2) since it forces one to recognize the limits of the original languages and our own language, it

Perhaps I misunderstood my professor in my first exegesis class, who himself seemed to have great confidence in this method of historical-grammatical exegesis. I probably should have gotten a hint that I had misunderstood him when, in another class, he disagreed with my exegetical conclusion in my term paper but said I supported it well enough to get a good grade on the paper. But I operated from what I thought he said, and so this fear of missing *the* right interpretation often left me with little to say, other than attacking the interpretations of others.

In case you are rendered paralyzed by the need to be correct always, I want to encourage you to speak boldly and confidently, even if you know your word is not the last word. Indeed, given the long, long history of students of the Bible who have intensely studied the text, wrestled with it in all sincerity, and come away with different interpretations, your word can hardly be the last word. This does not mean that some interpretations are not more probable (even far more probable) than others and that some are completely wrong, but it does mean that we have to recognize that coming to *the* unassailable, right meaning for all time is beyond our abilities, if for no other reason than the original authors are dead and cannot be questioned on the ambiguities. And since times change and social and congregational contexts change, neither can we find *the* once-for-all meaning for our day and for future generations.

---

invites humility against overly-confident assertions about God from the text; (3) the "best reason" is "reading in the original languages slows us down, and reading the text more slowly is essential for learning to love the Bible."

We take seriously the task of exegesis out of love for God, because we want to know him better and love him more deeply and because we want others to do the same. We take the task seriously in order to rule out unlikely or even heretical readings and to aid our understanding of possible meanings of the text, but that still leaves a lot of room for options. We also take the task seriously because we are attempting to speak the word of God to people, many of whom may actually act on what we say.

But if we wait to arrive at the perfect understanding, one that we will never change our minds about or that cannot be contradicted by others, we will never speak. We believe that we are saved by grace through faith in Jesus Christ (Ephesians 2:8), not by perfect biblical interpretation. We need to allow the grace of God to cover our teaching and preaching of the Bible as well, because our interpretations bear the marks of our imperfections and fallen state. Many of you will be called to preach and teach. So take the task seriously, prayerfully struggle with the text to hear a word, and then boldly speak it, allowing the congregation to discern God's word in your words.[2]

2. For what it is worth, I have found two of Karl Barth's essays in *The Word of God and the Word of Man*—"The Need of Christian Preaching," and "The Task of the Ministry"—helpful in overcoming my reluctance to speak but also realizing the seriousness of the task.

21

Don't Voice All of Your Thoughts or Doubts

ONE OF my most frightening moments as a new teacher
came when I was teaching a class called "Critical
Introduction to the Bible" to undergraduate Bible majors,
many of whom intended to become ministers. This class deals
with the origins of Scripture, how scholars look at the Bible,
and the nature of biblical inspiration. Most of our students
come out of conservative church backgrounds and view matters related to the Bible from a fairly conservative standpoint.
The class tended to open up a number of questions for such
students and called into question long-cherished beliefs.
Others, however, latched onto these "new" perspectives with
gusto and wanted to share these views with everyone. What
alarmed me was that one of these students told me that she
was sharing the class material with the youth group at the
church where she was an intern.

My fear was that she had not sufficiently had time to
process all she was learning. She did not yet really know
what she believed, so it seemed to me both naïve and ir-
responsible to pass on information to teenagers who were
even less equipped to deal with such matters. Furthermore,
although I did not hear whether it actually caused a stir at her
church, I was afraid that she did not take into account what

the parents of these kids might think about this novice youth minister teaching these things to their children. Parents have an instinct to protect their children's faith from things that they think could undermine it. Thus, I started advising my students in this class to hold their tongues in church on many of the things we raised in class until they had time to think them through.

The motives for such sharing vary. Some, like the student above, just wanted to pass on new information out of excitement. Others like to blow people out of the water by lobbing controversy at them (a most unloving motivation!), or they simply delight in voicing new ideas that make them feel smart (another unloving motivation). Some think out loud and so process the information in front of others. This is fine before teachers or peers, but such a practice can damage the faith of the "uninitiated" or have them write you off as being either wishy-washy or too radical or untraditional (or perhaps even too traditional in some cases).

Some students also use teaching opportunities to voice their own questions or doubts that have been raised by their studies. "I'm not sure if the Bible is historically reliable." "Paul may not have written this letter." "Things are more ambiguous in the Greek, so I do not know if we can really understand this text all." Questioning and struggling are natural parts of theological education and should be, and they certainly have a place in the church as well. There will always be ambiguity when talking about the things of God or the content of books passed down over centuries, copied and recopied, and translated in different languages (i.e., the Bible). But if every time you speak before fellow Christians you consistently offer a litany of things you do not know, do not understand, or are not sure about, then you will do little good for those seeking to understand *something* about Jesus and his expectations for his disciples.

What to do then? If doubts or questions are serious, it may be a time to avoid teaching roles in the church, at least until some matters are more settled for you.[1] However, some internships or other roles require students to preach or teach in church. So, if you are simply awash in new ideas and views that you have not yet sorted out, teach on subjects that are more certain to you. And by all means, keep in mind that if your education is causing confusion and doubt for you—if you try to simply pass on everything you are learning, unprocessed in your own mind—imagine the confusion and doubt your teaching can cause your hearers.

Finally, even once you have settled your mind on various issues, you still need to ask whether it is worthwhile to share this information in church. That is, you do not have to teach everything you think or know or think you know. I am not suggesting that you lie about your understanding of certain matters if asked. However, you do not have to introduce every thing you know or think you know unless, in as much sincerity, love, and humility you can muster, you think it is important and beneficial for nurturing the faith of God's people in your church.

---

1. Thielicke is more forceful on this point, insisting that first-year seminary students are not to preach because of this unsettledness in their own theological understanding. *A Little Exercise for Young Theologians*, 12.

22

Don't Be a Visionary

"WHERE THERE is no vision the people perish"
(Proverbs 29:18, KJV). This verse has become the
mantra of many who see themselves as visionaries for the
church, those who are convinced that they can rescue the
church from the current crisis, which threatens its very survival. To listen to much of what is said in the books, pulpits,
blogs, and seminary classrooms, the church is always in some
dire crisis or another. Thus, some will claim, what is needed
is someone who can see ahead and lead the church into its
bright tomorrow. If the older generation will not do it (and
they probably cannot because they are likely considered the
cause of the crisis or accomplices in it), then it is up to the
up-and-coming generation of pastors and teachers to show
the way. Loaded with ideas of what the church "ought to be"
and certain of their own ability to lead it there, they begin
to lay out their plan for revival. This plan or vision is culled
from bits and pieces of inspiring lectures, select and often
decontextualized Bible verses, popular books on how to grow
churches, and the visionaries' own innate sense, which has
been honed by their newly acquired theological skills. They
believe themselves called to be a new Moses, leading the people out of bondage to old thoughts and ways; a new David,

slaying whatever giants oppose the progress (as they define it) of the church and laying plans for a new temple of God; a new Peter, converting the masses on a new Pentecost; a new Paul refusing to allow old traditions to constrict the gospel; a new Jael, driving spiritual stakes through the hard heads of the enemies who oppose them.[1]

Without denying the possibility that God could indeed call you to this, it is at least worth noting that God does not often call those who are expecting or intending to do great things. He goes after the unlikely: the fugitive shepherd, whose picture is plastered on "Wanted" papyri all over Egypt; the young shepherd and musician, whose brothers see him as a trouble-maker and whose king sees him as a usurper; the quick-speaking but often slow-witted fisherman; the sickly persecutor of Christians who, after his conversion, raises a ruckus in almost every town he enters; the stay-at-home wife in her tent. David could be considered a dreamer as he lays the plans for God's temple, but keep in mind that God told David that a temple was unnecessary and that David was not the one to build it anyway (2 Samuel 7:1–16).

The problem here is not lacking the faith that God can do great things through individuals, even you. God has done and still does great things through individuals. The problem arises in two other areas. First, there is the hubris of thinking that you know what is best for the church and that somehow or other everyone else is doing it wrong. This is not—I repeat this is *not*—denying that there are problems in the churches and the fact that some churches are doing things wrong. In

1. If you are not familiar with these allusions, see, respectively, Exodus 11–15, 1 Samuel 17, Acts 2, Galatians (among others for Paul), and Judges 4–5.

fact, it is probably true to say all churches are doing some things wrong. The issue, rather, is envisioning yourself as the one who is going to rescue the church from itself—that you are going to save it with your grand vision of how things ought to be done. *The church already has a Savior, and it is not you or me.* The hubris becomes even more evident if you consider yourself a martyr because everyone cannot see the divine wisdom in your vision.

Second, the definition of "great things" is tricky. Typically we would consider great things for Christ to be things like starting huge social programs that help many people, preaching revivals that convert hundreds, growing big churches (compare 1 Corinthians 3:6), or becoming a nationally recognized Christian leader. All of these things might indicate that God is at work, but none of them are either necessarily good or the work of God. A good test might be whether the focus is consistently on the person behind these things or on God.

Despite our understanding of "great things" as large-scale, well-known, and impressive, it seems to me that "great things" for God are more often realized through those who do things like serving churches day in and out, visiting the sick and those in the nursing homes, sharing their hope and faith with the person beside them on the plane, taking food to the poor under the bridge, and giving a cup of cold water in the name of Jesus (Matthew 10:42). None of these may get any notice, which is perfectly consistent with the call of the kingdom of God (Matthew 6:1–4), and, when they do get noticed, the deeds glorify the One who sends rather than the one sent (Matthew 5:13–16).

There are times and places where the church needs a course correction, and God *may* have called you as a voice for change. If called in this way, your role may be large or may go unnoticed. But, such a need is usually better discerned within a community immersed in Scripture and by those whose dedicated service to the church over time has earned them a hearing. Dietrich Bonhoeffer, in *Life Together*, argues, "God hates visionary dreaming." Why?

> . . . it makes the dreamer proud and pretentious. The man who fashions a visionary ideal of community demands that it be realized by God, by others, and by himself. He enters the community of Christians with demands, sets up his own law, and judges the brethren and God Himself accordingly . . . When things do not go his way, he calls the effort a failure. When his ideal picture is destroyed, he sees the community going to smash. So he becomes, first an accuser of his brethren, then an accuser of God, and finally the despairing accuser of himself.[2]

Bonhoeffer concedes that such dreams may arise from "honest and earnest and sacrificial" intentions, but such intentions do not mitigate the destruction caused by one who, in Bonhoeffer's words, "loves his dream of a community more than the Christian community itself."[3] So rather than complain about the church and make plans for turning the church into what we think it should be, Bonhoeffer says we are to receive the church, as is, as a gift of God.[4] I think this understanding is helpful. Just as it would be the height of ingratitude to tell someone their gift is not good enough for

2. Dietrich Bonhoeffer, *Life Together* (San Francisco: Harper San Francisco, 1954), 27–28.

3. Ibid., 27.

4. Ibid., 28.

us or could be improved, so our response to what we see as faults or shortcomings in the church can reflect ingratitude toward God.

This returns us then to Proverbs 29:18, which is better translated "Where there is no *revelation*, people cast off restraint" (TNIV). That is, the vision talked about in this proverb is not a modern concept of vision as long-range planning and foresight. Rather "vision" here is a word often used of prophetic vision, that is, a revelation *from God*. In this proverb, "vision" has nothing to do with charting the success, the "great things," for the future of God's people. It has to do with keeping God's people on the course that *God* has laid out for them, restraining them from going in their own ways. And there is the key: The vision for the church and the future of the church is God's, not ours, and God is certainly able to see it through. The church desperately needs prophetic voices to draw people into God's vision for the church, but what is incumbent upon us is to first submit ourselves to *God's* vision and leading rather than baptizing our own vision as God's.

PART FOUR

Final Exhortations

23

Be Appreciative

W HEN I graduated with my first master's degree, my dad made a joking comment about being glad I was through because my schooling was getting expensive. Initially, I was insulted by this because I had worked hard, saved my money, and got my degree on my own. Or so I thought. I had let it slip my mind that one summer during that time, my dad let me work for him (at far higher pay than anyone else doing the same job would have made) and that I lived with my parents that summer to save money. Hmmm. Maybe I did not do all of this on my own after all, any more than I did it all on my own when I mowed yards for money as a teen. Sure I pushed the mower, but Mom and Dad had bought the mower, and the car I carried the mower in, and the gas can I filled up, not to mention the clothes I worked in.

As time went on, my indebtedness to others became more obvious. When I married, my wife, Amy, took on full-time work, often in jobs she hated, in order to put food on the table and pay the bills so I could pursue my studies. She did this in spite of ongoing fatigue and pain, which we later discovered was because she has lupus. She did all this because she sees herself as a partner in a shared ministry, but she clearly got the worse end of the partnership for a number of years. Then there was that Thanksgiving one year, when we lived in student housing and money was tight. Thanksgiving morning we found an envelope that someone slid under our apartment door. In it was $75, not much by some accounts, but a lot to us at that time. We suspect the older couple who lived next door, but if so, they never said a word. From time to time checks would arrive from our parents or cash or gift cards would come from friends. My gut instinct at one time would have been to send it all back. But my wise dad reminded me that given the ministry I was entering, the ministry of teaching, I would have to learn to accept help at times. What I have learned to do is gratefully accept such gifts. So despite my past pride in being a Lone Ranger theological student, it has now become clear to me how many hands were involved in my theological education.

My guess is that your theological education has similar patron saints, perhaps your parents or grandparents, your spouse, friends, or your home church. Therefore, my plea here is simply that you be appreciative and show that appreciation to those who have played a role in your theological education. Recognize that many people are involved in your preparation for ministry, many who are in fact partners in your ministry, and who are enabling you to fulfill your calling. How marvelous a gift of God! So say, "Thank you" and praise God. Moreover, since others are investing in your education and ministry, take them seriously.

Beyond family and friends, keep in mind as well the whole network of people at your school who have a hand in your education. Appreciate the teachers in your classrooms, who often could make better money elsewhere, but who are there because of their own sense of calling. Be thankful for the administrators who make the school run day to day. True, you may not always agree with how the school is run, but I suspect that only a few days in the administrators' shoes—having to deal with budgets, purchasing, logistics, alumni relations, fundraising, scheduling, and so on—would heighten your appreciation for what they do. Especially, show your gratitude to those people we often ignore and who make even less (often much less!) than the teachers and administrators, namely the people who maintain the facilities, clean your classrooms and bathrooms, who cook your food, and who haul your trash out. What a shame if we overlook these wonderful people even as we train to be servants in Christ's church. Remember as well those donors to your school, who make it possible for you to get your education for far less than what it actually costs. These are the men and women who throughout the history of your school have given generously, often sacrificially, because they believe in the mission of the school, some of whom have their names on buildings but most of whom do not.

Each year during my MDiv program I was asked to write a note of thanks to the woman who sponsored my scholarship, and I think this was a marvelous practice not only to show appreciation to her, but also to instill a discipline of appreciation in me. Beyond such gestures, for the many unknown and unnamed donors and for the contributors to your education that you do know, the best way to honor and appreciate their gifts is to take your theological education seriously.

24

Charge to a Graduating Class[1]

I CONSIDER it a great privilege to have been asked to address those receiving bachelor's degrees in Bible and those receiving master of arts and master of divinity degrees. At first, I could not figure out why I was asked to do this. Maybe it has to do with how much joy and how many fond memories my "Critical Introduction to the Bible" class has generated over the last few years. Whatever the reason, I am glad to have this opportunity.

The other theological faculty members and I have been honored to be your teachers and have enjoyed the relationships we have developed with you over the last few (or for some of you, several) years. We look forward to continuing the friendships. It is our hope that we have well equipped you with the necessary tools for your lives of ministry, whether in service to a church or in some other calling.

It is our prayer that, empowered by the Spirit of God, you will use these tools as well as your gifts and your zeal

1. On May 10, 2003, I delivered the following address to undergraduate Bible majors, who were graduating from Lipscomb University's College of Bible and Ministry, and graduate students graduating from Lipscomb University's Hazelip School of Theology. I thought it was a fitting way to end this book. I have made only minor changes to my original manuscript.

to serve our Lord, his kingdom, and his world in a way that brings glory to God's name.

This afternoon, I am drawing my comments from a passage that is fairly familiar to you—or should be after all this Bible education—John 13. Here Jesus does for his disciples what they were unwilling to do either for one another and, apparently, for their master; that job reserved for lowly slaves and the disciples of rabbis. But Jesus, knowing full well who he was, where he was from, and where he was going (v. 3), takes a basin of water and a towel and begins to wash his disciples feet. He is motivated by love for those with him, and he shows them his love fully.

What's more, in telling of this act of self-giving, the author of the Gospel of John anticipates Jesus's ultimate gift on the cross. The language of Jesus knowing "his hour had come" (v. 1) points to the cross. The description of Jesus laying down (v. 4) and taking up his clothes (v. 12) echoes his comments elsewhere in John about laying down and taking up his life (John 10:18). After Jesus completes this service, verses 12–17 continue:

> When he had finished washing their feet, he put on his clothes and returned to his place. "Do you understand what I have done for you?" he asked them. "You call me 'Teacher' and 'Lord,' and rightly so, for that is what I am. Now that I, your Lord and Teacher, have washed your feet, you also should wash one another's feet. I have set you an example that you should do as I have done for you. Very truly I tell you, servants are not greater than their master, nor are messengers greater than the one

who sent them. Now that you know these things,
you will be blessed if you do them."

Jesus charges his servants to live a life imitating his own self-sacrificing service. And today I simply want to remind you, as you live out your ministries, that you have been called to service, motivated by love for your master and by love for those you will encounter in your ministries. Thus, rather than thinking of ministry as we typically do today—as a profession or office—I encourage all of us to think of it in terms of function or action: to minister is to serve.

In order to serve like Jesus, we need to internalize, and then live out, those Kingdom qualities that Jesus mentions elsewhere: poverty of spirit, meekness, an insatiable desire for righteousness, mercy, and purity of heart. In addition, as the Apostle Paul argues, we must act in love, because all of our knowledge and gifts and service become meaningless apart from a love that seeks the good of others rather than of self.

So, please, do not get trapped in an attitude toward your ministry that it is somehow all about you and your advancement or even your pleasure. It is about service to God and others. Don't buy into the mindset that says the goal is to move on to bigger and better things—that says, "Sure I may have to start in a small, unexciting church, but that will just be a stepping stone to bigger and better things." Such thinking is in the spirit of self-service, not service to others. The goal is not, "movin' on up." The goal is dropping on down—to your knees—with a towel in one hand and a wash basin in the other.

Furthermore, there may be times in your ministry, in fact I'll guarantee you that there will be times in your ministry, when you are asked or required to do things that you will not enjoy. In fact, given the God of surprises we serve, you may find yourself as the next Moses or Esther or Jeremiah, who protests, "I didn't sign up for this! I am not up to it!" When aspects of your ministry do not produce immediate happiness, fulfillment, or satisfaction, you may be tempted to simply move on or call it quits—or at least complain and moan.

In such instances, I invite you to recall the image of Jesus's hands, holding those nasty feet, and the image of those same hands, pierced with nails. There is great joy in all ministries, but the joy comes in serving the One who has called us and recognizing that we are his agents for his purposes.

You may well find yourself at the table with the doubter, who will not believe it until he sees it. You may sit with the one you thought was your biggest supporter, but who, in the moment of greatest need, lets you down. Your table may include those who are seeking power and glory for themselves and who will defend their turf against you. You may end up sitting with those who simply do not understand what you are saying, no matter how many times and ways you explain it. You may discover you are eating with those who are not at all sure about you and ask, "Can anything good come out of a theological school?" You may find yourself at the table with the one who smiles to your face but then stabs you in the back.

That is, you may find yourself at a table very much like Jesus's table in John 13. And what did he do? One by one he lovingly served each of them, with a towel and wash basin, and later on the cross. You—we—are called by Jesus to do as he has done. As he tells the disciples and us, "I have set you an example that you should do as I have done for you" (v. 15).

God has blessed you with a wonderful opportunity; a chance to be a part of the growth and realization of his kingdom; a chance to imitate, indeed incarnate, the very life of Christ in sacrificial service. Embrace the call with eagerness and joy, imitating through your service the one we call Lord and Teacher. In the chapter on the discipline of service in his book *Celebration of Discipline*, Richard Foster says, "The risen Christ beckons us to the ministry of the towel. Such a ministry, flowing out of the inner recesses of the heart, is life and joy and peace."[2] To conclude with the words of Jesus, "Now that you know these things, you are blessed if you do them."

2. Richard J. Foster, *Celebration of Discipline*, rev. ed. (San Francisco: Harper San Francisco, 1988), 140.